First World War
and Army of Occupation
War Diary
France, Belgium and Germany

18 DIVISION
54 Infantry Brigade,
Brigade Machine Gun Company
8 February 1916 - 31 January 1918

WO95/2045/2

The Naval & Military Press Ltd
www.nmarchive.com
Published in association with The National Archives

Published by

The Naval & Military Press Ltd

Unit 10 Ridgewood Industrial Park,

Uckfield, East Sussex,

TN22 5QE England

Tel: +44 (0) 1825 749494

www.naval-military-press.com

www.nmarchive.com

This diary has been reprinted in facsimile from the original. Any imperfections are inevitably reproduced and the quality may fall short of modern type and cartographic standards.

© **Crown Copyright**
Images reproduced by permission of The National Archives, London, England, 2015.

Contents

Document type	Place/Title	Date From	Date To
Heading	2045/2 No 54 Brigade Machine Gun Coy		
Heading	18th Division 54th Infy Bde No. 54 Machine Gun Coy. Feb 1916 Jan 1918		
Heading	War Diary of No 54 Machine Gun Coy. from 8/2/16 To 290216 Volume 1		
War Diary	Grantham	08/02/1916	08/02/1916
War Diary	Holloway	08/02/1916	08/02/1916
War Diary	Southampton	08/02/1916	08/02/1916
War Diary	Havre	09/02/1916	12/02/1916
War Diary	Mericourt	12/02/1916	12/02/1916
War Diary	Franvillers	12/02/1916	29/02/1916
Heading	War Diary of No 54 Machine Gun Coy from 1.3.16 to 31.3.16 (Volume II)		
War Diary	Corbie	01/03/1916	05/03/1916
War Diary	Bray	06/03/1916	31/03/1916
Heading	War Diary of No 54 Machine Gun Coy from 1st April 1916 to 30th April 1916 (Volume III)		
War Diary	Bray	01/04/1916	30/04/1916
Heading	War Diary of No 54 Machine Gun Coy. from May 1916 to 30th June 1916 Volume		
War Diary	Bray	01/05/1916	03/05/1916
War Diary	Maricourt	04/05/1916	04/05/1916
War Diary	Oissy	05/05/1916	22/06/1916
War Diary	Bray	23/06/1916	30/06/1916
Map	Maricourt.		
Heading	54th Machine Gun Company. July 1916		
Heading	War Diary of No 54 Machin Gun Coy. from 1st July 1916 to 31st July 1916 (Volume VI)		
War Diary	Bray	01/07/1916	07/07/1916
War Diary	Bronfay Farm Bois-De-Tallies	08/07/1916	12/07/1916
War Diary	Trigger Wood Maricourt	13/07/1916	18/07/1916
War Diary	Bois-de-Tallies	19/07/1916	20/07/1916
War Diary	Neuville-de-Bois	21/07/1916	24/07/1916
War Diary	Eblinghem	25/07/1916	28/07/1916
War Diary	Meteren	29/07/1916	31/07/1916
Miscellaneous	Appendices I &II.		
Miscellaneous	Appendix I	08/07/1916	08/07/1916
Miscellaneous	Appendix II	17/07/1916	17/07/1916
Heading	War Diary of No 54 Machine Gun Coy. from 1st August 1916 to 31st August 1916 (Volume VII)		
War Diary	Meteren	01/08/1916	03/08/1916
War Diary	Armentieres	04/08/1916	22/08/1916
War Diary	Ervinghem	23/08/1916	24/08/1916
War Diary	La Thieuloye	25/08/1916	31/08/1916
Heading	War Diary of 54 M.G. Coy from 1st Sept 1916 to 30th Sept 1916		
War Diary	Thieuloye	01/09/1916	16/09/1916
War Diary	Raincheval	17/09/1916	25/09/1916
War Diary	Authville	26/09/1916	28/09/1916
War Diary	Thiepval	29/09/1916	30/09/1916

Heading	War Diary of No. 54 Machine Gun Coy from 1st Oct 1916 to		
War Diary	Authville	01/10/1916	15/10/1916
War Diary	Beauval	16/10/1916	16/10/1916
War Diary	Vardencourt	17/10/1916	18/10/1916
War Diary	Albert	19/10/1916	31/10/1916
War Diary	Pozieres	01/11/1916	01/11/1916
War Diary	Albert	02/11/1916	27/11/1916
War Diary	Drucat	28/11/1916	14/12/1916
War Diary	Donvast	15/12/1916	31/12/1916
Heading	War Diary of 54 Machine Gun Coy from 1st Jan 1917 to 31st Jan 1917		
War Diary	Donvast	01/01/1917	11/01/1917
War Diary	Berneuil	12/01/1917	14/01/1917
War Diary	Rebeampre	15/01/1917	15/01/1917
War Diary	In Trenches	16/01/1917	27/01/1917
War Diary	Martinsart	28/01/1917	31/01/1917
Heading	War Diary of 54 M.G. Company from 1st Feb 1917 to 28th Feb 1917		
War Diary	Martinsart	01/02/1917	28/02/1917
Miscellaneous	Appendix I		
Heading	War Diary of 54 Machine Gun Company from 1st March 1917 to 31st March 1917		
War Diary	Bouzincourt Authille	01/03/1917	26/03/1917
War Diary	Thiennes	27/03/1917	31/03/1917
Heading	War Diary of 54 Machine Gun Company from 1st April 1917 to 30th April 1917		
War Diary	Thiennes	01/04/1917	20/04/1917
War Diary	Le Pire	21/04/1917	26/04/1917
War Diary	Sachin	27/04/1917	27/04/1917
War Diary	Neuville Vitasse	28/04/1917	30/04/1917
Heading	War Diary of 54 Machine Gun Company from 1st May 1917 to 31st May 1917		
War Diary	Neuville Vitasse	01/05/1917	12/05/1917
War Diary	N.31 C.	13/05/1917	31/05/1917
Miscellaneous	Appendix No.1	10/06/1917	10/06/1917
Heading	War Diary of 54 Machine Gun Company from 1st June 1917 to 30th June 1917		
War Diary	N.31 C.	01/06/1917	02/06/1917
War Diary	Hindenburg Support	03/06/1917	17/06/1917
War Diary	Monchy-Au-Bois	18/06/1917	18/06/1917
War Diary	Pas	19/06/1917	28/06/1917
War Diary	Monchy-Au-Bois	29/06/1917	30/06/1917
Heading	War Diary of 54 Machine Gun Company from 1st July 1917 to 31st July 1917		
War Diary	Canal Reserve Camp (H27.b.5.6)	01/07/1917	12/07/1917
War Diary	Steenvoorde	13/07/1917	16/07/1917
War Diary	Buysscheure	17/07/1917	31/07/1917
Miscellaneous	Appendix. I.		
Heading	War Diary of 54 Company Machine Gun Corps from 1st August 1917 to 31st August 1917		
War Diary	Pas	01/08/1917	03/08/1917
War Diary	Godwarveldte	04/08/1917	06/08/1917
War Diary	Dickiebusch	07/08/1917	22/08/1917
War Diary	Whippenhoek	23/08/1917	23/08/1917
War Diary	Winnezeele	24/08/1917	28/08/1917

War Diary	Whippenhoek Dickiebusch Huts	29/08/1917	29/08/1917
War Diary	Canal Reserve Camp	30/08/1917	31/08/1917
War Diary	Buysscheure	01/09/1917	03/09/1917
War Diary	Ledringhem	04/09/1917	22/09/1917
War Diary	Tunnelling Camp	23/09/1917	30/09/1917
Heading	War Diary of 54 Company Machine Gun Corps from 1st October 1917 to 31st October 1917		
War Diary	Tunnelling Camp	01/10/1917	11/10/1917
War Diary	Irish Farm	12/10/1917	13/10/1917
War Diary	Tunnelling Camp	14/10/1917	16/10/1917
War Diary	Irish Farm	16/10/1917	19/10/1917
War Diary	Chateau De Trois Tours	20/10/1917	22/10/1917
War Diary	Irish Farm	23/10/1917	25/10/1917
War Diary	Dirty Bucket Camp	26/10/1917	29/10/1917
War Diary	Partridge Camp	30/10/1917	31/10/1917
Heading	War Diary of 54 Company Machine Gun Corps from 1st November 1917 to 30 November 1917		
War Diary	Partridge Camp	01/11/1917	05/11/1917
War Diary	H Camp International Corner	06/11/1917	09/11/1917
War Diary	Emile Camp Elverdinghe	10/11/1917	17/11/1917
War Diary	H Camp International Corner	18/11/1917	22/11/1917
War Diary	H Camp	22/11/1917	22/11/1917
War Diary	Emile Camp Elverdinghe	23/11/1917	28/11/1917
War Diary	Box Camp A.S.C. 9.1	29/11/1917	30/11/1917
Operation(al) Order(s)	Corrigenda To Operations Order No. 22		
Heading	War Diary of 54 Company Machine Gun Corps from 1st Dec 1917 to 31st Dec 1917		
War Diary	Box Camp A.S.C. 9.1	01/12/1917	05/12/1917
War Diary	Larry Camp Rear H.G.	06/12/1917	11/12/1917
War Diary	Box Camp A.S.C. 9.1	12/12/1917	15/12/1917
War Diary	Portsmouth Camp	16/12/1917	17/12/1917
War Diary	Haringhe Area X. 24.a.5.5	18/12/1917	31/12/1917
Heading	War Diary of 54 Company Machine Gun Corps from 1st Jany 1918 to 31st Jany 1918		
War Diary	Houlle	01/01/1918	04/01/1918
War Diary	Box Camp	05/01/1918	10/01/1918
War Diary	Larry Camp Trenches	11/01/1918	17/01/1918
War Diary	Box Camp	18/01/1918	23/01/1918
War Diary	In Trenches	24/01/1918	30/01/1918
War Diary	Crombeke	31/01/1918	31/01/1918

2045/2 No 54.
136 Bft Brigade Machine
Gun Coy.

18TH DIVISION
54TH INFY BDE

NO. 54 MACHINE GUN COY.

FEB 1916 - JAN 1918

CONFIDENTIAL.

WAR DIARY

OF

No 54 MACHINE GUN COY.

FROM 8/2/16 TO 29/2/16

(VOLUME 1.)

WAR DIARY
or
INTELLIGENCE SUMMARY
(Erase heading not required.)

Army Form C. 2118

Instructions regarding War Diaries and Intelligence Summaries are contained in F. S. Regs., Part II. and the Staff Manual respectively. Title Pages will be prepared in manuscript.

Place	Date	Hour	Summary of Events and Information	Remarks and references to Appendices
GRANTHAM	9.2.16	a.m. 3.30	Started entraining in SOUTH DOCK GRANTHAM STATION.	
"	"	4.15	Entraining completed; long time due to horses, mules, limbers & men all being at different platforms	
"	"	5.5	Left GRANTHAM.	
HOLLOWAY	"	8.30	Arrived. Horses & mules watered.	J.M....
"	"	9.0	Left.	
SOUTHAMPTON	"	p.m. 1.35	Arrived.	
"	"	2.45	Disembarkation completed.	
"	"	4.30	Left in NORTHWESTERN MILLER (FURNESS LINE)	
HAVRE	9.2/10.2.16	a.m. 1.30	Arrived Somewhat nearing.	
"	"	9.30	Started disembarking.	
"	"	p.m. 12.15	Marched off to NO 1 REST CAMP (SANVIC CAMP)	J.M....
"	"	2.0	Arrived at Camp. Wigwam fire	
"	10.2.16		Still in Camp. ? 1 private evacuated to Hospital	J.M....

Army Form C. 2118

WAR DIARY
or
INTELLIGENCE SUMMARY
(Erase heading not required.)

Instructions regarding War Diaries and Intelligence Summaries are contained in F. S. Regs., Part II. and the Staff Manual respectively. Title Pages will be prepared in manuscript.

Place	Date	Hour	Summary of Events and Information	Remarks and references to Appendices
HAVRE	11.2.16		Still in camp. Received orders at 1 p.m. to entrain same day 9pm	
"	12.2.16	A.M. 8.30	1st & 2nd Coy. entrained as Pte. 3 GARE du MARCHANDISE	
"	"	9.0	2nd " " " "	
"	"	10.30	1st " " " "	
"	"	12 noon P.M.	2nd " " " "	
"	"	8.30	1st " " " " (R.H.Q.= FRANCE train 62D [illeg])	
"	"	10.15	2nd " " " "	
FRANVILLERS	13.2.16 12 midnight	1st " " " arr billets (R.H.Q. " " ")	yes
"	13.2.16	6 am	2nd " " " Billets [town]	
"	"	3.30	Still in billets	
"	"		" " "	yes
"	29.2.16		Weather bad - snow frost + rain	

1875 Wt. W 593/826 1,000,000 4/15 J.B.C. & A. A.D.S.S./Forms/C. 2118.

54 MG Coy
Vol 2

XVIII

CONFIDENTIAL.

WAR DIARY

OF

No 54 Machine Gun Coy.

From 1.3.16   to 31.3.16

(Volume II.)

WAR DIARY / INTELLIGENCE SUMMARY

Army Form C. 2118

Place	Date	Hour	Summary of Events and Information	Remarks and references to Appendices
CORBIE	1.3.16	12.30pm	Left FRANVILLERS. Ref. map "FRANCE" 62D First edition Scale 1/40,000	
		4.0pm	Arrived at CORBIE. BILLETS good. Two stragglers on march. 4½ miles long.	
"	2.3.16		Visited trenches N.E. of CARNOY (Ref. map. Trench map MARICOURT 62c N.W.1)	
"	3.3.16		Routine work. Received orders to move to BRAY on 6.3.16.	
"	4.3.16		Routine work.	
"	5.3.16		Routine work.	
BRAY	6.3.16	3.30pm	Left CORBIE	
		6.0pm	Arrived BRAY. March Sever.	
BRAY	7.3.16		Took over Trenches E. of CARNOY from 21st Bde M.G.C.	
	8.3.16		Routine work.	
	9.3.16		Routine work.	
	10.3.16		Routine work.	
	11.3.16		Routine work.	
	12.3.16		Routine work.	
	13.3.16		Routine work.	
	14.3.16		Routine work.	
	15.3.16		Routine work.	
	16.3.16		Routine work.	
	17.3.16		Routine work. 2/C KENNARD admitted to hospital. Weather fine	P.S.

Army Form C. 2118

WAR DIARY
INTELLIGENCE SUMMARY
(Erase heading not required.)

Instructions regarding War Diaries and Intelligence Summaries are contained in F. S. Regs., Part II. and the Staff Manual respectively. Title Pages will be prepared in manuscript.

Place	Date	Hour	Summary of Events and Information	Remarks and references to Appendices
BRAY.	18.3.16		Routine work. Weather fine	R.S.
	19.3.16		" " " "	PKR
	20.3.16		Routine work. Weather fine 4834 Pte MURDOCH evacuated to HQ	PKR
	21.3.16		Routine work. Weather fine	PKR
	22.3.16		Routine work. Rain	PKR
	23.3.16		Routine work. Snow & frost.	PKR
	24.3.16		Routine work. Snow & blizzard. Thaw & frost at night	PKR
	25.3.16		Routine work.	PKR
	26.3.16		Routine work. Rain	PKR
	27.3.16		Routine work. Weather dull	PKR
	28.3.16		Routine work. Weather fine	PKR
	29.3.16		Routine work. Weather fine	PKR
	30.3.16		Routine work. Weather fine	PKR
	31.3.16		Routine work. Weather fine 2Lt- ALMOND 2Lt- Attewell killed.	PKR

SECRET
54. M.G. Coy
Vol 3

18th

CONFIDENTIAL.

War Diary

Of

No 54 Machine Gun Coy.

From 1st April 1916.   To 30th April 1916.

(Volume III)

WAR DIARY
INTELLIGENCE SUMMARY
(Erase heading not required.)

Army Form C. 2118

Instructions regarding War Diaries and Intelligence Summaries are contained in F. S. Regs., Part II. and the Staff Manual respectively. Title Pages will be prepared in manuscript.

Place	Date	Hour	Summary of Events and Information	Remarks and references to Appendices
BRAY	1st		Still in trenches N.E. of CARNOY. Situation Normal.	Ref. Appendix No. 1.
"	2nd		1 man admitted to hospital	"
"	3rd		"	"
"	4th		"	"
"	5th		"	"
"	6th		"	"
"	7th		"	"
"	8th		"	"
"	9th		"	"
"	10th		"	"
"	11th		"	"
"	12th		"	"
"	13th	2am	GERMANS various trenches in A9a & A9a were sullen & intermittently shelling started at our wire between front line in A9a. M.G's opened fire & caused heavy enemy. trenches in A9a were not shelled & members entered at a.m. on cemetery in enemy. Enemy situation normal.	Ref. Appendix No 1.
"	14th		Still in trenches N.E. of CARNOY. Situation normal.	"
"	15th		"	"
"	16th		"	"
"	17th		"	"
"	18th		"	"

Army Form C. 2118

WAR DIARY
or
INTELLIGENCE SUMMARY

(Erase heading not required.)

Instructions regarding War Diaries and Intelligence Summaries are contained in F. S. Regs., Part II. and the Staff Manual respectively. Title Pages will be prepared in manuscript.

Place	Date	Hour	Summary of Events and Information	Remarks and references to Appendices
BRAY	19th		Still in trenches N.E. of CARNOY. Situation normal.	
"	20th		" "	
"	21st		" "	
"	22nd		" "	
"	23rd		" "	
"	24th		" "	
"	25th		" "	
"	26th		" "	
"	27th	1.30 a.m.	GERMAN lines opposite A1 + A2 (communicated from 15 minute Machine Gun bursts on trenches & German trenches at A 9 b 55.65 + A 7 b 97.27	
"		1.35 a.m.	M.G. bursts ceased.	
"		1.45 a.m.	Two enemy patrols attempted to rush GERMAN line at A 9 b 55.65. this busy failed — seen at A 7 b 97.27 — this party succeeded.	
"		1.50 a.m.	Machine Gunner Lewis Gunner ceased.	
"		1.55 a.m.	Gunner ceased.	
"		2.00 a.m.	Ceased.	

Place	Date	Hour	Summary of Events and Information	Remarks and references to Appendices
BRAY	27th		M.G's firing were allotted tasks following pts. Bigneep. SILLERY.N/w MARICOURT A9 a10.15.05; A9 a 10.50; 2 guns in FLEURE at A 9 a 2.3. 1:10.000. A 9 a 15.10 ; A8 b 25.15; A8 u 45.05; A7 d 2.8. Our two guns incessantly on approaches from MONTAUBAN. 2 hostile M.G's which opened fire on (French) French tk in neither case were silenced immediately they gave away their whereabouts & were silenced afterwards by the enemy. No casualties was suffered by the Coy(?)	
BRAY	28th		Still in trenches N.E. & CARNOY. Situation normal. 1 man wounded by M.G. fire	
"	29th		" " " " " " 1 O.R. wounded by M.G fire Situation normal.	
"	30th		Still in trenches N.E. of CARNOY. GERMANS bombarded our line heavily about 6.30 p.m. 2/Lt. LESLIE PHILIP PEARCE badly hit in right front & back by shell. 10.R. owing to 2/Lt. PEARCE hit badly in thigh by shell fire. Otherwise situation normal. JCem(?)	

18 May-June
54 M.G. Coy

"A" BRANCH,
HEADQUARTERS,
18th Div.
No. 78/87
Date 18 SEP 1916

CONFIDENTIAL Vols. 4.5

WAR DIARY
OF
N° 54 MACHINE GUN COY.

MAY 1916
FROM 1st ~~JUNE~~
TO 30th JUNE 1916
(VOLUME)

receipt acknowledged
22.9.16
aw

Army Form C. 2118

WAR DIARY
or
INTELLIGENCE SUMMARY
(Erase heading not required.)

Instructions regarding War Diaries and Intelligence Summaries are contained in F. S. Regs., Part II. and the Staff Manual respectively. Title Pages will be prepared in manuscript.

Place	Date	Hour	Summary of Events and Information	Remarks and references to Appendices
BRAY	1-5-16		A.9. D Nicholas holding front line. B section in support at CARNOY. C. Section in reserve at BRAY. Situation normal. Died of wounds Pte NICHOLAS	
	2-5-16		Situation normal	
	3-5-16		—do—	
MARICOURT OISSY	4-5-16	2 a.m.	Relieved by 6/9 M.A.Coy. 4-15 a.m. Reached MARICOURT LOCK & entrained for PICQUIGNY at 1-15 p.m. Transported by road via CORBIE	
	5-5-16	10.25am	To watermill at PICQUIGNY & marched to OISSY	
	6-5-16		Cleaning of Kit. 2 p.m. Inspection by Coy Officer	
	7-5-16		Usual Routine Work in Billets	
	8-5-16		—do—	
	9-5-16		—do—	
	10-5-16		Field day. Tactical Handling	1 O.R. admitted to Hospital
	11-5-16		—do—	
	12-5-16		Range	1 O.R. admitted to Hospital
	13-5-16		Combined drill under Company Officer	
	14-5-16		Field day. Company inspected at Work by Servant for temp. Coy Officer	
	15-5-16		Scheme to seize of a Village	
	16-5-16		—do— Tactical Handling	
	17-5-16		Range	
	18-5-16		Usual Routine Work in Billets. Inspection of Livestock by Coy Officer	Lieut P.K. PAUL granted leave to U.K. Lieut H.R. WHITTINGTON Reinforcement
	19-5-16		—do—	
	20-5-16		—do—	
	21-5-16		—do—	
	22-5-16		—do—	2 O.R's Reinforcements
	23-5-16		Field day. Tactical Handling. 8 O.R's.	Capt. Groves granted leave to U.K.
	24-5-16		—do— Support of Infantry in attack	—do—
	25-5-16		—do— —do—	
	26-5-16		Usual Routine Work in Billets & Range	Sergt Gotowem granted leave to U.K.
	27-5-16		—do—	
	28-5-16		Field day. Support of Infantry during an attack	
	29-5-16		—do— Tactical Handling	
	30-5-16		—do— Defence of a Village	
	31-5-16		—do—	MAJOR J.C.N. MATHESON granted leave to U.K.

W. H. Greenough. Lt.

Army Form C. 2118

WAR DIARY
or
INTELLIGENCE SUMMARY
(Erase heading not required.)

Instructions regarding War Diaries and Intelligence Summaries are contained in F. S. Regs., Part II. and the Staff Manual respectively. Title Pages will be prepared in manuscript.

Place	Date	Hour	Summary of Events and Information	Remarks and references to Appendices
OISSY	1-6-16		Inspection of a Village in conjunction with Divn Guno	
	2-6-16		— do —	
	3-6-16		Field day, attack on a wood	
	4-6-16		— do —	See syllabus in Appendix
	5-6-16		— do —	
	6-6-16		Range practice, stoppages	Ycaed. O.S.O KOHNSTAM granted leave to U.K.
	7-6-16		— do — — do —	— do —
	8-6-16		Horse Parade. Work in Fields	C.S.M. R. Taylor granted leave to U.K.
	9-6-16		— do —	
	10-6-16		— do —	
	11-6-16	2 p.m.	Regt. arrived at ST.CHRISTE FARM for Brigade Training	Lieut. O.R. admitted to the hotel. One R.R. posted sick to U.K.
	12-6-16		Erecting of Bivouacs Etc	
	13-6-16		Bivouack, field days Practicing the attack	
	14-6-16		— do —	
	15-6-16		— do —	
	16-6-16		— do —	
	17-6-16		— do —	
	18-6-16		— do —	
	19-6-16		— do —	
	20-6-16		— do —	
	21-6-16		— do —	
	22-6-16		Horse Parade, work in fields	
	23-6-16	6.15 p.m.	Entrained at AILLY-SUR-SOMME. Detrained at HEILLY 6.45 a.m. & marched to BRAY	
BRAY	24-6-16	3 p.m.	Three sections proceeded to trenches at CARNOY a head over from PT.M.G.COY. Preliminary bombardment begun.	
	25-6-16		B section post him. A. Sa. CAFFET WOOD, D&Cd CARNOX C/m BRAY.	2nd C.B.r. Wounded Yeard/M.J.FISHER admitted to Hospital
	26-6-16		— do —	line O.R. — do —
	27-6-16		— do —	6m O.R. — do —
	28-6-16	4 p.m.	D section relieved by A section, otherwise positions unchanged	1m O.R. — do —
	29-6-16		— do —	Shelling heavy comes again
	30-6-16	3 p.m.	C sec. relieved by D. Sec. Two guns of C. Sec. to CAFFET WOOD a base to front line. Ycaed Mr.R. KENNARD Killed	Ycaed O.S.O. KOHNSTAM Killed. 2nd R admitted to Hospital. One O.R. Wounded

W.R. [signature]

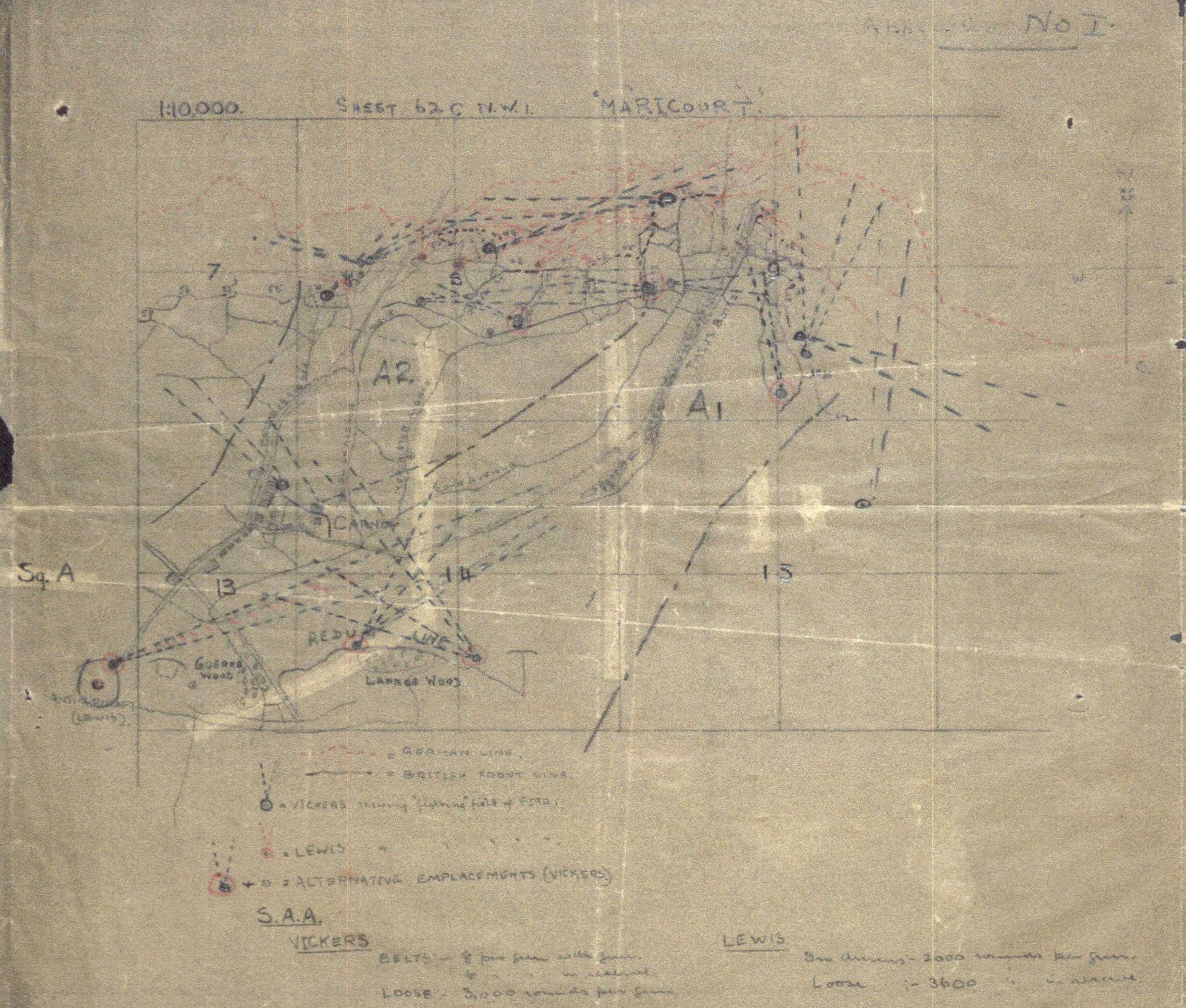
Appendix No I
1:10,000.
SHEET 62 C N.W.1
"MARICOURT"
Sq. A
7
8
9
13
14
15
A1
A2
CARNOY
GUERRE WOOD
REDU LINE
LAPREE WOOD
ANTI-AIRCRAFT (LEWIS)
= GERMAN LINE.
= BRITISH FRONT LINE.
= VICKERS showing "fighting" field of FIRE.
= LEWIS " " " "
+ o = ALTERNATIVE EMPLACEMENTS (VICKERS)
S.A.A.
VICKERS
BELTS :- 8 per gun with gun.
4 " " in reserve
LOOSE - 3,000 rounds per gun.
LEWIS
In drums - 2000 rounds per gun.
Loose :- 3600 " in reserve.

54th Inf.Bde.
18th Div.

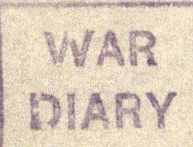

54th MACHINE GUN COMPANY.

JULY

1916

Attached:
   Appendices I & II.

54 MGC

18

July. Vol 6

CONFIDENTIAL

WAR DIARY

OF

No 54 MACHINE GUN COY.

(VOLUME VI)

FROM 1st July 1916   TO 31st July 1916

WAR DIARY or INTELLIGENCE SUMMARY

Army Form C. 2118

(Erase heading not required.)

Instructions regarding War Diaries and Intelligence Summaries are contained in F.S. Regs., Part II. and the Staff Manual respectively. Title Pages will be prepared in manuscript.

Place	Date	Hour	Summary of Events and Information	Remarks and references to Appendices
BRAY	1-7-16	7.30 am	Attack on German trenches at CARNOY. Casualties O.R's 2 killed, 16 Wounded.	See Appendix I
	2-7-16		4 Guns in reserve on battlefield part Nos. 2,3 in case pltn. W in rear of 96th Bde. 14th Bn.Rifle Brigade. 16th Bn.R.B. 2 Guns pltn.W.S.I. Casualties 5 O.R's wounded.	— do —
	3-7-16		— do —	— do —
	4-7-16		1am. Mr. P.H. WHITE TRENCH B.26 A.1.2.1.5am. spoken. L.M.P TRENCH + MONTAUBAN ALLEY. 5am. 2am./5th. Pln. on CATERPILLAR TRENCH. Remainder of Positions unchanged.	— do —
	5-7-16		2 Guns moved up to CATERPILLAR TRENCH to relieve CATERPILLAR MARLBRO WOOD. Remainder of Positions unchanged.	— do —
	6-7-16		J.Section normal	— do —
	7-7-16		— do —	— do —
			Casualties 2 O.R's killed	
BRONFAY FARM	8-7-16	6 pm	Company relieved by 9th M.G.COY. & stayed the night at BRONFAY FARM. Wounds C.E.COD OH F.WHEELER Reinforcements H.F.Wheeler	
BOIS-de-TALLIES	9-7-16	4 am	Marched to BOIS-de-TALLIES Reinforcements 2 Y.G.O.CPM son	
	10-7-16		Cleaning up Etc.	
	11-7-16		— do —	
	12-7-16		Reinforcements 4 Y.G.O's	
TRIGGER WOOD	13-7-16	6.30 am	Marched to TRIGGER WOOD	See Appendix II
MARICOURT	14-7-16	1 am	Two sections of TRIGGER WOOD moved to MARICOURT. C Sections moved up to TRONES WOOD. B section to the BRIQUETRIE. L.und P.K.PAUL + Revd J.M.BENBOW Served. Officers II	
		2 pm	D. Section moved to DUBLIN TRENCH. A Section remained at MARICOURT. Reinforcements 30 Y.G.O.S 9 pm. Relieved 53 M.G. COY.	— do —
	15-7-16		4 Guns in DUBLIN TRENCH, 10 Guns TRONES WOOD + 2 Guns at the BRIQUETRIE Casualties O.R's 1 killed O.R. wounded	— do —
	16-7-16		Positions unchanged Casualties 3 O.R's wounded	— do —
	17-7-16		— do —	— do —
	18-7-16		Relieved by 115 M.G.COY. Two Guns of D Section remained at the BRIQUETRIE	— do —
BOIS-de-TALLIES	19-7-16		Two Guns of BRIQUETRIE relieved. Company marched to BOIS-de-TALLIES	
	20-7-16	10 am	Transport moved to NEUVILLE-au-BOIS via POINT NOYELLES	
NEUVILLE-au-BOIS	21-7-16	7.30 am	Entrained at EDGE HILL Station. Transport arrived NEUVILLE-au-BOIS 9 pm	
	22-7-16	7.30 am	Entrained at WIRY and marched to NEUVILLE-au-BOIS	
	23-7-16		Cleaning up Etc.	
	24-7-16	9 am	Marched to LONGPRÉE + entrained at 3 pm. Entrained at ARQUES 11.15 pm Sea moved up at the Station	
EBLINGHEM	25-7-16	12.30 am	Marched to EBLINGHEM arriving 6.15 am	5 O.R's admitted to Hospital
	26-7-16		Cleaning up Etc.	2 O.R's " "
	27-7-16		Us at Routine Work in Billets	2 O.R's " "
	28-7-16		— do —	2 O.R's " "
METEREN	29-7-16	10 am	March for METEREN	
	30-7-16		Small Routine Work in Billets	2 O.R. admitted to Hospital
	31-7-16		Field Coney Tactical Handling	

APPENDICES I & II.

WAR DIARY

Appendix I

Reference Dates 1st to 8th July, 1916

The disposition of the Guns during the preliminary bombardment was as follows:-

    1 Section (4 Guns) held the line with the 7th BEDFORDS
    1 -do- was in Reserve in CARNOY
    1 -do- was in CAFTET WOOD
    1 -do- was in BRAY

The Section in the line kept the Enemy Wire in front of AUSTRIAN TRENCH & AUSTRIAN SUPPORT open by firing in it continually at night

Two Guns from the Section in CARNOY kept the wire in front of EMDEN TRENCH, BUND TRENCH & BLACK ALLEY open by firing at night from positions in EDWARD AVENUE

The Section in CAFTET WOOD fired on BLACK ALLEY, POMMIERS TRENCH, BUCKET TRENCH & POMMIERS REDOUBT, keeping the wire open.

On the 1st July, the 4 Guns in CAFTET WOOD, with two Guns from the Section which had been in BRAY, gave covering fire - these two Guns had taken up a position on the PERONNE ROAD - as the Infantry advanced, firing in accordance with a time table and firing on a target south of BUND TRENCH

The remaining two Guns of the Section which had been in BRAY took up positions one in each of the RUSSIAN SAPS in the Brigade front about 60 yds. from the German front line. These Guns opened fire on the enemy position 5 minutes before ZERO & continued firing until masked by our own Infantry.

The Gun in the right Sap was blown from its emplacement 3 times by the concussion of our own Shells bursting on the German front line.

At ZERO, 4 Guns of "D" Section went forward with the 6th wave, 2 Guns under 2/Lieut HUMPHREYS with "A" Coy., 7th BEDFORDS & two Guns under 2/Lieut TELFER with "D" Coy. 11th R. FUSILIERS

These Guns moved with the 6th wave until MAPLE TRENCH & POMMIERS REDOUBT were reached. The two right Guns, i.e., those with the 7th BEDFORDS took up positions in POMMIERS REDOUBT, & the two left Guns pushed forward along BEETLE ALLEY with "D" Coy. 11th R. FUSILIERS & took up positions there. The left Gun of these two Guns wiped out a party of Germans who had been driven out of FRITZ TRENCH into the open

The Section in CARNOY advanced in the rear of & under cover of the 6th NORTHANTS and took up positions, two Guns in the strong point in POMMIERS TRENCH, one Gun in Strong Point No III & one Gun in Strong Point No II

The Gun in Strong Point No II got a direct hit shortly after it was in position with a 5.9 in. Shell. The Tripod was destroyed, the Gun put out of action

Appendix I Continued

temporarily - it had the barrel casing pierced - two of the Gun numbers killed and the Sergeant seriously wounded.

This Section was very ably led into action by Sergeant BUCKLEY - the Officer was killed the previous Day - who, although wounded early in the assault continued to command the Section until relieved 8 days later

"A" Section, which had been in CAFTET WOOD advanced at 8.15 a.m and with short halts made its way, two Guns to the POMMIERS REDOUBT, one Gun to Strong Point No I and one Gun to Strong Point No IV.

The two Guns in the RUSSIAN SAPS, with the two Guns which had been firing from the PERONNE ROAD, remained in our front line as Brigade Reserve

Little firing was done on the first Day - the Gun numbers being engaged in digging themselves in, in recognizing the ground, and in making range - cards.

The position then at the end of the first Day was:-

```
4 Guns in reserve in our old front line
2   "   "  Strong Point No IV
1   "   "      "     "   No III
1   "   "      "     "   No VI
2   "   "  POMMIERS REDOUBT
2 Guns in trench between "  " & MONTAUBAN ALLEY
1 Gun in Strong Point No V
2 Guns in BEETLE ALLEY
```

JULY 2nd The two Guns which were in position in the trench East of the REDOUBT moved up & occupied the Strong Points immediately in rear of WHITE TRENCH, & the Gun in No IV Strong Point moved up and took up a position in BEETLE ALLEY

The six Guns in BEETLE TRENCH & WHITE TRENCH kept all the ground behind FRICOURT constantly under fire. Good observation of fire was obtained. Most of the targets engaged were about 2,000 to 2,500 yards away and many of the enemy were seen to fall

In one instance, a party of Germans emerged from dug-outs near RAILWAY COPSE and proceeded in the direction of FRICOURT WOOD. These dug-outs had been previously ranged on and a Gun was immediately trained on to them. Many of them were seen to fall and the remainder scattered in various directions, some of them returning to the dug-outs again

On another occasion, transport on the road running from BAZENTIN-LE-PETIT WOOD to MAMETZ WOOD was fired on. One rider fell from his Horse and remainder broke into a gallop. This road was kept under fire every night as also was MAMETZ WOOD

JULY 3rd The same areas were kept under fire. QUADRANGLE SUPPORT

Appendix I Continued

had a lot of Traffic in it on this Day and was kept under constant fire. One Party walked alongside the Trench for a bit and then several dropped, and the remainder jumped into the Trench again.

JULY 4th On the evening of July 4th

- 1 Gun from the REDOUBT
- 1 " " Strong Point No V
- 1 " " " " No VI and
- 1 " " " " No III

were moved further East and took up the following positions:—

- 1 Gun in Strong Point in WHITE TRENCH about S.26.a.1.2.
- 1 " at junction of LOOP TRENCH & MONTAUBAN ALLEY
- The other two Guns took up position in the two Strong Points in CATPILLAR TRENCH

These Guns fired on the road running from BAZENTIN-LE-PETIT WOOD to MAMETZ WOOD and on the German 2nd Line.

The Gun in BEETLE ALLEY still fired on QUADRANGLE TRENCH and SUPPORT, and on the BAZENTIN ROAD.

One Gun moved with the 12th MIDDLESEX REGT. and took up position in MARLBORO WOOD

JULY 5th Two Guns were moved from BEETLE ALLEY to CATERPILLAR TRENCH and took up positions to defend CATERPILLAR WOOD & MARLBORO' WOOD. Fire was still kept up on MAMETZ WOOD, BAZENTIN ROAD and the German 2nd Line.

JULY 6th The Day was without incident — searching fire was still kept up

JULY 7th — do — — do — — do —

JULY 8th All Guns were relieved by the 9th M.G.COY.

Signed J.C.M. MATHESON

W.H.Genwood. Lieut.
Comdg. 54 M.G. Company.

WAR DIARY

Appendix II

Reference Dates. 14th to 17th July 1916

One Section under Lieut PAUL accompanied the 6th NORTHANTS to TRONES WOOD. This Section by 5 p.m., had 1 Gun in Strong Point A and two Guns at North end of TRONES WOOD.

The Guns already in position of 55 M.G. COY. were relieved, and on the evening of the first day the position was as follows:-

- 2 Guns at North end of TRONES WOOD
- 1 Gun in Strong Point A
- 2 Guns in MALTZ HORN FARM TRENCH
- 4 " " the BRIQUETERIE

Next Day, 6 Guns were moved up to TRONES WOOD and at the end of the Second Day the position was as follows:-

- 4 Guns in Reserve in DUBLIN TRENCH
- 10 Guns holding TRONES WOOD
- 2 Guns at the BRIQUETERIE.

On two mornings working parties were caught by fire from the Guns at Strong Point A. These working parties were in front of GILLEMONT. Otherwise nothing of hope happened.

Signed J.C.M. MATHESON

W. L. Jenwood Lieut.
Comdg. 54 M.G. Company

CONFIDENTIAL.

WAR DIARY

OF

No 54 MACHINE GUN COY.

FROM 1st August 1916   TO 31st August 1916

(VOLUME VII)

Army Form C. 2118

WAR DIARY
or
INTELLIGENCE SUMMARY
(Erase heading not required.)

Instructions regarding War Diaries and Intelligence Summaries are contained in F.S. Regs., Part II. and the Staff Manual respectively. Title Pages will be prepared in manuscript.

Place	Date	Hour	Summary of Events and Information	Remarks and references to Appendices
METEREN	1-5-16		Usual Routine work in Billets. 1 O.R. admitted to Hospital	
	2-5-16		—do— —do—	
	3-5-16		—do— Afternoon, Range	
ARMENTIERES	4-5-16	5-30am	Marched to LE CHAPLE d'ARMENTIERES. Transport to ERQUINGHEM	
	5-5-16	6-30pm	A,C,& D sections proceeded to the trenches & relieved Nº II M.G.Co.y. (ANZACS) 1 O.R. admitted to Hospital	
	6-5-16		A & D Sections holding front line. C Section subsidiary line. B Section in Reserve at ARMENTIERES	
	7-5-16		Position unchanged. Situation normal	
	8-5-16		—do—	
	9-5-16		—do—	
	10-5-16		—do—	
	11-5-16		—do—	
	12-5-16		—do—	
	13-5-16	5-30am	Relief carried out. B relieved A, A relieved C, C relieved D. Wound MAJOR J.C.M. MATHESON Wounded (Rifle Shot) 6-30pm	
				Temperature with sweat fire during the night
	14-5-16		B & C Section holding front line. A Section of subsidiary line. D Section in reserve at ARMENTIERES situation normal	Lieut E.C.T. MINET "Royal Fusiliers" assumed command of the Company
	15-5-16		Situation normal during the day. No enemy raid.	—do—
	16-5-16		Situation normal. —do— Enemy Barrage on German Front line	
	17-5-16		—do—	
	18-5-16		—do—	
	19-5-16	6-30pm	Relief carried out. A relieved B, D relieved A	1 O.R. admitted to Hospital
	20-5-16		A & D holding front line. B in subsidiary line. C in reserve at ARMENTIERES	Situation normal
	21-5-16		Situation normal	
	22-5-16		—do—	
ERQUINGHEM	23-5-16	10-30am	Company relieved by 102 M.G.Co.y. & marched to ERQUINGHEM. 1 O.R. admitted to Hospital	
	24-5-16		Cleaning up. Etc	
LA THIEDLOYE	25-5-16	1-30am	Marched to BAILLEUL & entrained for ST POL. detrained at 11-15am & marched to LA THIEULOYE	
	26-5-16		Cleaning up. Etc	
	27-5-16		Tactical handling	
	28-5-16		Usual routine work in Billets	Capt H. WILLIAMSON transferred from 125 M.G. Co.y.

Army Form C. 2118

WAR DIARY
or
INTELLIGENCE SUMMARY
(Erase heading not required.)

Instructions regarding War Diaries and Intelligence Summaries are contained in F.S. Regs., Part II. and the Staff Manual respectively. Title Pages will be prepared in manuscript.

Place	Date	Hour	Summary of Events and Information	Remarks and references to Appendices
LA THIEULOYE	29-8-16		Usual Routine. Work in Billets. Lieut W.L. JERWOOD transferred from GINGOX	
	30-8-16		Training with Royal Engineers under Capt CHASE. Consolidating newly won positions	
	31-8-16		13 Brigade Field Coy.	

W.L. Jerwood Lieut.
Comdg. 54 M.G. Company.

1875 Wt. W593/826 1,000,000 4/15 T.R.C. & A. A.D.S.S./Forms/C. 2118.

September 18 / Vol 8

CONFIDENTIAL

WAR DIARY

OF

54 M.G. Coy.

FROM 1st Sept 1916 TO 30th Sept 1916

WAR DIARY
or
INTELLIGENCE SUMMARY
(Erase heading not required.)

Army Form C. 2118

Instructions regarding War Diaries and Intelligence Summaries are contained in F.S. Regs., Part II. and the Staff Manual respectively. Title Pages will be prepared in manuscript.

Place	Date	Hour	Summary of Events and Information	Remarks and references to Appendices
THIEULOYE	1-9-16		The Company carried on the vicinity of the Billets. The morning was devoted to Gun cleaning & P.T. etc.	
	2-9-16		Special class of selected infantrymen instructed in gun work. Lectures & tactical exercise. Scheme defence of BOIS-DES-HERBAGES against enemy advancing from TINQUES, returning to Billets 5.30 p.m.	
	3-9-16		The Company on tactical exercise provided by the officers Nos 1, 2, 3 & 4 later had a game our march. The Commanding Officer's meeting was held afternoon. Usual Stables work in Billets. Appeared otherwise being forced to sleep in open without covers.	
	4-9-16		Brigade tactical exercise. Scheme – Advance guard moving and retreat of a worsted forces moving to move on Siebert.	
	5-9-16	3.30 a.m.	Orders received for proceeding the move forward. Company marched in Billets, & thoroughly overhauled all Saddlery & Gun Equipment	
	6-9-16	9.30 a.m.	Inspection of Capt. by Assist. General Montbridge. Lieut. MINET Mounted over the remainder of the Company to Capt. WILLIAMSON. Gun work in Billets, for remainder of day.	
	7-9-16		The Company remained in Billets during the morning. At 2 p.m. Company marched to B Training area & did a tactical exercise. Scheme support of infantry in attack.	
	8-9-16		Modern Officers selected their own positions, and later the G.O. inspected them and criticised.	
			The Company on C. training area all day. During the morning Platoon A&B practised intensive digging & the construction of lossett dug outs. The other ½ coy. advance the team & tactical handling of M.Gs in open warfare. The ½ Coy. changed round in the afternoon. Orders received to move on [?] Instead	
	9-9-16	8 a.m.	Marched to NEUVILLE-AU-CORNET. The march was made prepared. The Coy. went took the vicinity at the starting point Later the Column was inspected by the Lieut. General (Major General MAYSE) Established in Billets at 12.30 p.m.	
	10-9-16	10 a.m.	The march was continued. Reached SUS-ST-LEDGER 9.30 p.m. The march was 10 ½ miles one fall and leaving the march. Capt. WILLIAMSON's horse fell 9 times then hurt to the ground. He mixed outs on the night train & was a severe shaking. He was carried by the ambulance of the R. Fusiliers and later sent to a rest station at DOULLENS. Lieut. W.F. TERWED took over command.	
	11-9-16	7.30 a.m.	The move was continued to RAINCHEVAL. Ordered at the agreed of ST-LEDGER and drove to HALLOY. 6½ hours journey, delayed once after more delay due to 55 Brigade passing. Marched to new area. The distance was 10 ½ also 7 of which were marched. Company fed out. The transport was hopeless, arriving at 12 noon. Train in M.T.	
	12-9-16		The morning was devoted to Gun cleaning & Gun work. The Coy. did an exposed scheme in the afternoon.	
	13-9-16		Gun work in the vicinity of the Billets. In the afternoon special attacks was given to pushing Wireless. Set & Brass & thread camp splinters were tested & replaced.	
	14-9-16		Sections A & B did a tactical exercise during the morning. C & D fired dropping practice an arc improvised range. After dinner C Coys changed round.	
			The O.C. under Private arrangements visited the area recently captured from the enemy in the vicinity of OUILLERS & POZIERES.	
	15-9-16		Sections A & B spent the morning in intensive digging in. The training area. C & D continued with dropping & practical on Range. R boys changed round after dinner.	
	16-9-16		Small tactical exercises by Sections during the morning of final attention being paid to the attack. In the afternoon all the coys taken over put into one squad for reformed musketrees, the remainder had 2hrs gun drill and a short march.	

1875 Wt. W593/826. 1,000,000 4/15 J.B.C. & A. A.D.S.S./Forms/C. 2118.

WAR DIARY or INTELLIGENCE SUMMARY

Army Form C. 2118

Place	Date	Hour	Summary of Events and Information	Remarks and references to Appendices
RAINCHEVAL	17-9-16		The Adjt. General expressed the wish that the Officers should have a rest. Officers had the opportunity of attending services of the various denominations. Lieut. E.G.T. MINET 11th R. FUSILIERS took over command of the Company.	
	18-9-16		Tactical exercise arranged but cancelled owing to heavy rain. Lecture on Anti-gas Protection & Practice on fitting helmets & instruction in same work after 10.30 am.	
	19-9-16		Platoons out in the open all morning doing tactical schemes. The afternoon was devoted to preparing clothing and arm cleaning.	
	20-9-16		Capt. ½ Coy. practical intensive sniping, the construction of temp. cover M.G. emplacements. The right ½ Coy. did open work in open country specially particular attention to moving of positions quickly and crossing rough ground and obstacles.	
	21-9-16		Reveille at 5. The officers all day tactical handling.	
	22-9-16		Capt. D. was attached to 11th R.FUS. to practise the attack. Trenches were laid out on the latest proportions. The remainder of the Coy. had a competition in intensive digging. Each set of three men had one pick & one shovel, one foot marked out 6' x 2'6". The men working them in record 55 cubic feet in 35 mins. In the afternoon inter-section sports took place and were given away at night. Operations arranged for 8 to 11 pm — were carried on account of broken lamp refused to move. On the following day they arrived at MEDAUVILLE reached the outskirts of wood. Those dinner & reached HULA.302 — when refugees tiny and clear of village. We marched 3 Plats — each gave four accommodation for the officers.	
	23-9-16	7-30 a.m.	In the morning games were always & everything prepared for the forthcoming battle. It was that I took for the remainder of troop orders, received 5.30pm to march at 8am to AUTHUILLE Packed and ALBIUS WOOD per lorries & men handled the boxes from there to point to the NORTH BLUFF.	
	24-9-16		Soft rain, we were shelled before days and accommodation was of mediocre sort. The Officers at one Officers mess was renovated.	
	25-9-16		Attack on THIEPVAL. 6 ON 2 a.m. final orders were received. ZERO hour fixed for 12.35. — All troops had to be employed in trenches beforehand. 9th 10th 11 were to attack the ridge where on our position. 15 GREEN with 2 Guns of O.Sec. with the 1st Coy of the momentary Battalion W. TELFER with 2 Guns of D.Sec. with H. Wells of the 17th Army Coy. 18 officer Wd WHEELER with G Sec was in support. The momentary ½ Battalion of 9th D. were kept as reserve in THIEPVAL WOOD under John NELDER & WALLACE W. GODD with 2 Guns. Each w. position on the ridge between HAMEL & MESNIL with usual for supplying ammo at all to follow the attacking troops on march. H4 4 forward guns were placed to form a support line near the CHATEAU. Wd. TELFER was killed and no O.Rs. was lost, 2 killed 9 11 wounded. Any of the Lewis guns got carried on along by the 8th & leading the morning in course of 7 field turns was established at the CHATEAU. Lt. Wd NELDER & team of the Guns were relieved by the morning by Sec. of C.Sec under Sd. CODD who replaced Wd. NELDER (who L. Regt. Fld) by Sd. WALLACE. Carriers 1 O.R. wounded.	
	26-9-16		Carry the morning C. & GREEN Sec was bad schemes were relieved by A. Sec from the MESNIL ridge. 10th ½ — attack continued to be less pushed from the opposition to the ridge. Wd. WALLACE with 2 Guns of D.Sec. went forward with the succeeding Battn. & brought back gun into action on the important bit. The whole of SCHWABEN REDOUBT was not taken but on crossing a message that the Bty dug in was consolidated by Bd. CODD getting forward with the 2 gun teams. No position in support, 135° behind our front line, during the morning Wd. WHEELER with 2 guns of O.Sec. was forward to a ploughed comm in support of Wd. CODD. Other guns were moved from THIEPVAL WOOD the Lincoln 200 yards north of the CHATEAU. Those last 4 guns were not used but kept in the trenches ready for immediate action.	

1875 Wt. W593/826 1,000,000 4/15 J.B.C. & A. A.D.S.S./Forms/C. 2118.

WAR DIARY
or
INTELLIGENCE SUMMARY

(Erase heading not required.)

Army Form C. 2118

Instructions regarding War Diaries and Intelligence Summaries are contained in F.S. Regs., Part II. and the Staff Manual respectively. Title Pages will be prepared in manuscript.

Place	Date	Hour	Summary of Events and Information	Remarks and references to Appendices
THIEPVAL	29-9-16		The enemy made a counter attack on the left at 10.30 a.m. & the Infantry were driven back. A number of the left about guns were assembled & remainder were forced to retire bringing with them the books of the Pems Offmeng. The gun opposed fell into the hands of the enemy. 2nd Lt WALLACE was killed during this action. 2nd Lt DODD took charge of the stargun of D section & the remains of the front team during the day & Sgt. was managed by [illegible] ga[v]e & had to be replaced from B section. Casualties 4 O.R.'s. Wounded	
	30-9-16		2nd Lt DODD had a accurate gun put out of action by shell fire & another gun was well apt from B section 184 Inf Bn were attack made on the northern side of the SCHWABEN REDOUBT. The Infantry on the right made good & N°55 M.G. Coy got 2 guns forward but the attack on our front failed. Our guns returned to their original positions. Casualties 4 O.R.'s. Wounded.	

W. L. Gemmell. Lt.
5th M.G.C.

Vol 9

CONFIDENTIAL

WAR DIARY

OF

No 54 MACHINE GUN COY

FROM: 1st Oct 1916 TO: 31st Oct 1916

WAR DIARY or INTELLIGENCE SUMMARY

Army Form C. 2118

(Erase heading not required.)

Instructions regarding War Diaries and Intelligence Summaries are contained in F. S. Regs., Part II. and the Staff Manual respectively. Title Pages will be prepared in manuscript.

Place	Date	Hour	Summary of Events and Information	Remarks and references to Appendices
AUTHUILLE	1-10-16		The shelling of THIEPVAL continued all day. One of His Guns on our front line was damaged by shell fire & had to be replaced by one of the support Guns. The enemy made no counter attack. Let sent bombing attacks continued all day in the SCHWABEN REDOUBT. Our Infantry were unable to clear the northern trenches of the REDOUBT.	
	2-10-16		The Guns on the THIEPVAL sector were relieved by 55 M.G.Coy during the morning. The 3 damaged Guns and the Gun equipment was carried out, but life covers were handled over at 11 a.m. Lt. JERWOOD took charge of 2 Guns of 'A' Section opposite THIEPVAL WOOD & 2 Guns of B from the same were taken over relieved 2 Guns of Y.COY in THIEPVAL WOOD. Our specialists were taken over on the front line & two Guns kept in Reserve at COY. H.Qrs.	
	3-10-16		The 4 Guns in THIEPVAL WOOD were under a heavy shell fire all day & the Guns of the Yorks Regiment were kept in the mouths of the dug-out. Three Guns were under the orders of the 55th Fd. Bde. The dust was very trying to the Heavy bombardment all day. No unusual occurrence.	
	4-10-16			
	5-10-16		Relieved by 117 M.G.Coy. The chief unarranged to start at 9a.m. but the relieving Teams did not arrive until 2p.m. & then relieved patrols made their way to the transport lines at HEDAUVILLE & occupied the old Huts. Rest/equipment & established in Billets 5.30 p.m. All under orders of 55 BDE.	
	6-10-16		The Coy moved back to rail Billets. The journey started at 11.30a.m. under XX MINET & entrained at ACHEUX for CANDAS & rejoined & marched to Billets at BERNEUIL. The Transport under MI. STERWOOD moved by road and rested for the night at RAINCHEVAL.	
	7-10-16		Coy rested. The transport marched from RAINCHEVAL at 6 a.m. & reached BERNEUIL at 1 p.m.	
	8-10-16 11 afn.		Inspection by Brigade Commander. Cancelled at 1-10 p.m. but all ranks underwent cleaning and one equipping for the day.	
	9-10-16		Continued a brushing up programme. Instead handing during the morning Company and open drill in the afternoon.	
	10-10-16		Schemes defence of LANCHE	
	11-10-16		Tactical handling on B area	
	12-10-16			
	13-10-16		Remained in vicinity of Billets. Found over the Equipment & thoroughly overhauled the Gun Teams	
	14-10-16		Outpost scheme in LANCHE VALLEY during the morning Company & others drill in the afternoon.	
	15-10-16 9 a.m.		Tactical exercise Lt. Co in attack. Orders received at 5 p.m. to move to westward night afterwards exercises in consequence	
BEAUVAL	16-10-16 6.30 —		Marched to BEAUVAL under O.C. NORTHAMPTONS.	
WARDENCOURT	17-10-16		Marched to WARDENCOURT. Halt for 2 hrs, at noon to allow outgoing troops to get clear of the village.	
	18-10-16		Left The Earl of CALEDON took command of the Company. We marched at 9 a.m. to a bank on the west side of DOUZENCOURT. Accommodation poor but safe bivouacs	
ALBERT	19-10-16 7 a.m.		Platoons Coy'd marched to POZIERS to assist T.3 Coy in the attack on REGINA TRENCH. Heavy rain necessitated the postponement of operations & Coy returns marched to ALBERT. The remainder of the Coy marched at 5-30 a.m. & Hts were in Billets at ALBERT at noon.	
	20-10-16		Inspection of Gun & equipment & Schools. In the afternoon the Coy marched to MAMETZ & inspected several old German M.G. emplacements	
	21-10-16		'C' & 'D' Company under Lt. Linton out for tactical handling Maj. the Coy. Instead at 5pm	
	22-10-16		Remainder of men bathed. Church parade at 10 a.m. O.E. & 2 Section officers made a reconnaissance of the line north of POZIERS	
	23-10-16		Half the Coy relieved 32 Coy in the line. 'C' Section took up its positions in REGINA TRENCH & 'D' were in reserve in McDONNELL TRENCH	

Army Form C. 2118.

WAR DIARY
or
INTELLIGENCE SUMMARY
(Erase heading not required.)

Instructions regarding War Diaries and Intelligence Summaries are contained in F. S. Regs., Part II. and the Staff Manual respectively. Title Pages will be prepared in manuscript.

Place	Date	Hour	Summary of Events and Information	Remarks and references to Appendices
ALBERT	24-10-16		Remainder of Coy. moved up to POZIERS. Transferred of Coy. then Coy. remained at ALBERT	
	25-10-16		When "D" relieved "C" in REGINA TRENCH & "C" & "B" returned to ALBERT. A remnant of Coy. 4th R.C. took up position in VANCOUVER TRENCH at night	
	26-10-16		REGINA TRENCH heavily shelled all day. Lieut. Ellis damaged & the equipment knocked early in the morning	
	27-10-16		A section D - 2nd in REGINA TRENCH & "D" withdrew to VANCOUVER TRENCH	
	28-10-16		Capt. McKay, Lieut. Ellis & 2"D" marched from ALBERT & 2.S. & 2.P. to POZIERS & "B" relieved "D" in REGINA TRENCH. 2" & relieved D in VANCOUVER trench. Third A.O.S. relieved in billets in ALBERT	
	29-10-16		Remained day. Operations again stopped. Arranged positions for Coy. waited for long cart on present lines	
	30-10-16		Trench refused in Coys advance in COURCELETTE ROAD be A. used by Lewis and present trenches. Heavy machine burnt air invited into carrots on the positions & then advanced against	
	31-10-16		Arrangements made to got dug out inshoeal for the front game, but the weather made it impossible to carry it forward.	

M. R. Jenwich
Lt. Adjt.
54 m. g. c.

WAR DIARY or INTELLIGENCE SUMMARY

Army Form C. 2118.

54th Machine Gun Coy T

Place	Date	Hour	Summary of Events and Information	Remarks and references to Appendices
POZIERES	1-11-16		Company relieved by 53 M.G.Coy. "A" Section was relieved by 4th & 1st 53 Coys to occupy ZOLLERN TRENCHES at 6am about 4pm. Taken into new type of Light H.Q.Q. & remainder of Coy returned to POZIERES in ALBERT Coy were billeted for cleaning Guns & Equipment	
ALBERT	2-11-16		Section "D" relieved "A" on ZOLLERN TRENCH	
	3-11-16		Company occupied with Sen drills. Preparations made in the afternoon for going into the Line.	
	4-11-16		The Coy relieved 53 Coy. in the Line "A" "B" went into the VANCOUVER TRENCH & "C" into REGINA TRENCH. Coy H.Qrs. took over the BELL-DUG-OUT near POZIERES CEMETRY. Coy. "D" was relieved by a sec. of 53 Coy. & returned to billets in ALBERT	
	5-11-16		Coys "B" & "C" changed over in REGINA & VANCOUVER TRENCHES as on 2 Guns in R. TRENCHES were in a very bad state & guards of REGINA impossible. Relief had to be carried out over the tops of posts.	
	6-11-16		The 1/2 Coy at ALBERT relieved the 1/2 Coy in the 2nd line. "A" to REGINA & "D" to VANCOUVER. The remains returned returned to billets at ALBERT	
	7-11-16		Day uneventful occurrence	
	8-11-16		Remainder of Coy H.Qrs. heavily bombarded with Gas shells. Casualties normal. Casualties 1 O.R. Wounded	
	9-11-16			
	10-11-16		Coy. relieved by 53 Coy. Relief started at midnight of the last Sec. marched ALBERT at 9am. Reliefs were arranged to arrive the Men from POZIERES to ALBERT	
	11-11-16		Coy. Inspection & cleaning of Guns & Equipment.	
	12-11-16		Relief commenced of 53 Coy in the Line. "C" & "D" Sections of ALBERT at 10am arriving at POZIERES at 1230pm. That Section then went & 4:30. Proceeded to the trenches to relieve 53 Coy in REGINA & VANCOUVER TRENCHES. Relief completed 4pm	
	13-11-16		Disposition unchanged. Artillery activities on both sides.	
	14-11-16		"A" + "B" Sections to ALBERT at 4:30pm. "C" + "D" Sections on arrival at POZIERES about 230pm Limbers moved & rested at "C" + "D" Sections commenced at 4:30pm. "C" + "D" Sections were accommodated in Coy. site.	
	15-11-16		Orders received that Coy would be relieved by Canadians on the 16/17/16. "D" Section arrived & proceeded to ALBERT arriving 4pm	
	16-11-16		Relief in progress, had not completed until 11-4am	
	17-11-16		The Coy at ALBERT. Orders received to be ready to move off on Three's notice	
	18-11-16 9am		Inspection by Coy. Officer	
	19-11-16 9am		Bath Parade. 10am. Kit inspection by all Section. Some of Guns of 5 section & the Men guns of D. the afternoon.	
	20-11-16		Commencement of a 4 days march. Coy ALBERT at 10:15am & marched to WARLOY	
	21-11-16		Parades at 9:30am & marched to HERISSART	
	22-11-16		" " 9 15am " " DOULLENS	

WAR DIARY
or
INTELLIGENCE SUMMARY

(Erase heading not required.)

Army Form C. 2118.

Place	Date	Hour	Summary of Events and Information	Remarks and references to Appendices
	24.11.16		Paraded at 7.15am and marched to GORGES	
	25.11.16	9am	" " " DONQUEUX	
	26.11.16	9.15am	" " " ST. RIQUIER	
	27.11.16	9.15am	" " " DRUCAT	Inspection by Divisional General on the march.
DRUCAT	28.11.16		Cleaning up & fitting of Clothing	
	29.11.16		Inspection and overhauling of Limbers	
	30.11.16	9am	Cap. Cadill 11am. Insp Gas Officers Inspection	

A. Wheeler 2nd Lieut
Comdg 57th M.T. Company

WAR DIARY or INTELLIGENCE SUMMARY

Army Form C. 2118

54. M.G. Coy
Vol XI

Place	Date	Hour	Summary of Events and Information	Remarks and references to Appendices
DRUCAT	1.12.16		Exercises on ST. RIQUIER training area	
	2.12.16		— do —	
	3.12.16		Church parade	
	4.12.16		Church parade & inspection of Billets by Company Officer	
	5.12.16		Company fitted all day with fighting limbers on ST. RIQUIER training area, finishing the annual	
	6.12.16		— do —	
	7.12.16		— do —	
	8.12.16		— do —	
	9.12.16		— do —	
	10.12.16		Church parade & inspection of Billets by Company Officer	
	11.12.16		Field day under Brigade arrangements. Battery Half attacked on PETIT MIRAMENT	
	12.12.16		Exercise of the gunners. Baggy weather that cancelled carrying so gas not weather	
	13.12.16		Brigade field day under the same arrangements as yesterday. 11th Preparations made for move to DONVAST	
	14.12.16		Paraded at 7.45am & marched to DONVAST. Billet accommodation very poor.	
DONVAST	15.12.16		Company holt. Reported training & cleaning.	
	16.12.16		No active work possible owing to heavy rain. Teachers on instruction to subject given to billets	
	17.12.16		Church parade & inspection of billets by Company Officer.	
	18.12.16		Coys. doing physical drawing & musketry of limbers	
	19.12.16		Coys. doing a tactical travelling.	
	20.12.16		Baths, issue of clothing & musketry & gun cleaning	
	21.12.16		Repulse shooting & blanket stoppages on the range	
	22.12.16		Y.W.C.A. day. Dinners at DONVAST after moved from same.	
	23.12.16		Company dance. Remainder shooting & all cleaned.	
	24.12.16		L. Coy. Y. Corps standby in the green — do —	
	25.12.16		X Mas day. O.C. Company dinner was served up to the y.ers, concluding with a most enjoyable concert	
	26.12.16		Head march to ST.RIQUIER training area	
	27.12.16		Lecture return of a parade on the official by Lt. Col. Stanley Clarke, commanding 2nd Cavalry Brigade.	
	28.12.16		Routine work and visible work	
	29.12.16		Routine work and Billets carry to Village	
	30.12.16		Company also shifted from DONVAST to billets at MILLANCOURT	
	31.12.16		Billet very dirty and officers of men have registered	

Vol 12

CONFIDENTIAL
WAR DIARY
OF
54. MACHINE GUN COY.

FROM 1st JAN. 1917
TO 31st JAN. 1917

Army Form C. 2118.

WAR DIARY
or
INTELLIGENCE SUMMARY

(Erase heading not required.)

Instructions regarding War Diaries and Intelligence Summaries are contained in F. S. Regs., Part II. and the Staff Manual respectively. Title Pages will be prepared in manuscript.

Place	Date	Hour	Summary of Events and Information	Remarks and references to Appendices
DONVAST	1-1-17	10 a.m.	Practising stoppages on the Range. A very wet day also, extra heavy rain to the day on followed with a very rough French dog-team land storm of snow.	
	2-1-17	5.45 a.m.	Practised loading up the guns, and entrenching digging.	
	3-1-17			
	4-1-17	9 a.m.	½ Coy marched to LE CROTAY. 2. LE CROTAY arriving abt 1½ h. marched to barricade where successful rifle Bombs of Coys came at 11. 9 classing of barricade arriving at Nov? 6 Coy of LE CROTAY returned to Bivouac about 5.30. 6. Rifle ins 2½ m.	
	5-1-17		Practising of stoppages. introduced to classing of guns. NOTE 2nd Lt 12.5 handed over to 2nd Lt. A.A.	
	6-1-17	8.4.9 a.m.	Gun drill. Practising of stoppages, rifle and target gunners rifle.	
	7-1-17	10 a.m.	Church parade. 2½ hours. Later in the day at 2 p.m. of A Coy 3 SIT MB COY 9 officers gave rating to a guide? a rover	
	8-1-17	8.45 a.m.	Practise bomb drill. 1st Lewis Transport inspected by Brigadier General Refreshment of tra in drawn up.	
	9-1-17		General drill to motor	
	10-1-17	9 a.m.	Coy marched by sections to L. hour intervals to CANCHY for Baths. 2 x clean clothing issued. Afternoon Rest.	
	11-1-17	10-15 a.m.	Marched to DONQUEUR arriving about 2.30 p.m. Every to Buck down of Peter to rest on the ditches.	
BERNEUIL	12-1-17	10-15 a.m.	" BERNEUIL " 1.30 p.m. in times moved up immediately on arrival. Blankets across stretching	
	13-1-17	9.30 a.m.	Paraded in full marching order for inspection of Equipment. It rained very hard. ½ O. FUSILIERS,	
	14-1-17	10-15 a.m.	Every to day under ½ R.F.O. did not move off until 10.45 a.m. for REBEAMPRE. The rate of the march for the latter part of journey was irrid the Company marching bo league files. Arrived REBEAMPRE 5.30 p.m.	
REBEAMPRE	15-1-17	8.45	Marched to ½ REBEAMPRE did aid not leave until 9.30 a.m. Everything cold funeral. arrived AVELUY 2.30 p.m. Commenced	
IN TRENCHES	16-1-17		to enter driving party to tackoturns, but by first 4½ officered the firemen Refered. 152 M.Coy. Relief completed 2.30 a.m. Constitution of the 16 Sector. Nich inference, the 3½° S.E. Redoubt. J.A. R26 c5. 2.18 m. R22 b. 7.7.2 m. R22 b 6.5.1.3 m. R22 b 12.3 m. R22 c. 24.1 am. R21 b 4.3.1 am. R21 a 9.4.1 bm. R20 b 8.8 bm. R22 c. 4.4. 2 am. R27 d 6. 7.5. 15m. R22 d.6. 15m. 9 sections New Dues or MOUQUET FARM	
	17-1-17		Position unchanged. Situation normal. Enemy airre 9 minute in most in evidence.	
	18-1-17	"		
	19-1-17	"	Shelby of coke moved forwarding of wire to each turn.	
	20-1-17	"	Own O.P. slightly wounded by shell fire	
	21-1-17	"		
	22-1-17	"		
	23-1-17	"		
	24-1-17	"		
	25-1-17	"	Commuspion 2 O.R. initial (aide of 53 M.G. COY.) 2 O.R.s. Wounded	
	26-1-17	"		
MARTINSART	27-1-17		Relief commenced by 53 M.G. COY 4.30 p.m. Relief completed 9.30 p.m. Marched to Hut near MARTINSART arriving about 11.30 p.m.	
	28-1-17	9.30	Paraded for Preparation by Coy Officer. Inspection first off until 11 a.m.	
	29-1-17	9.30 a.m.	followed by a Route march	

2449 Wt. W14957/M90 750,000 1/16 J.B.C. & A. Forms/C.2118/12.

Army Form C. 2118.

WAR DIARY
or
INTELLIGENCE SUMMARY

(Erase heading not required.)

Instructions regarding War Diaries and Intelligence Summaries are contained in F. S. Regs., Part II. and the Staff Manual respectively. Title Pages will be prepared in manuscript.

Place	Date	Hour	Summary of Events and Information	Remarks and references to Appendices
MARTINSART	30-1-17	9.30	Inspection by Section Officers & route march. Work commenced of putting huts & forw. under the huts.	
	31-1-17	9.30	" " cleaning of Guns & Equipment.	

E.Minns Capt.
Comdg. 172 M.G. Company

No. 14/13
Nov 1917
Feb 1917

CONFIDENTIAL

WAR DIARY

OF

54 M. G. COMPANY

FROM 1ST FEB. 1917 TO 28TH FEB 1917

WAR DIARY
or
INTELLIGENCE SUMMARY

(Erase heading not required.)

Army Form C. 2118

Place	Date	Hour	Summary of Events and Information	Remarks and references to Appendices
MARTINSART	1-2-17	9.30a	Parade for Inspection by Colonel. Officers followed by a check of arms and ammunition.	
	2-2-17		10-11 Physical Training. Company Commander of day to hold a morning parade.	
	3-2-17		10-12.30 — Foraging Parties.	
	4-2-17	10a	Church Service for all Religions	
	5-2-17	9.30a	Moved forth. Parade and Co's own to regt'l orders.	
	6-2-17		arms Cleaning. Orders received for position in trenches if emergency arose.	
	7-2-17	10a	Parade for situation of position of platoons in trenches of emergency.	
	8-2-17	9.30a	Cross Country Running, followed by notice 5 In G. Coy and 7 Co's stretcher bearers, followed with Gen. hdqts.	
	9-2-17		19 platoons marched off at 2.30p.m under lieut. Cogg. Coy took over at 3 p.m. — Relief of 1st R. Iniskg by 1st R.I.R.	
	10-2-17		... Position of coy 1st R.I.D53, 1st R.I.Y. Dn 5,2.R 12,22,B93, 2.R 22, 22,A95, 1st RJT D53, 1st RS C.75, 2.3 RS 94.5 RS 194. Hg: W.G in DOUQUET FARM	
	11-2-17		ditto of Coy commands 4,9 — Bde, Hg: bde 11.304.—	
	12-2-17	11a	Parade for inspection by Company Officers. Remainder of day for cleaning and necessary Co's Eqpts.	
	13-2-17	9.30a	Paraded and route march with Cavts. for field of goll.	
	14-2-17			
	15-2-17		208 Packs issued to Drivers at 3p.m — 2 to 7 to - all 3 Coys —	
	16-2-17		So Summits. attached to Reconnaissance made for the company attack	
	17-2-17		attack on ourselves front. Commenced at 11.51a.m.	
	18-2-17		So trench pocket occupied by O.E.M.A.Corp.	
	19-2-17		completion of Relief moved to MONMOUTH HUTS AVELEY. Moved to BERTO to DOUZINCOURT. Battalion passed very bad night	
	20-2-17	9.30a	Day spent in cleaning offing. Both were kept up for the fireman. Gas Casing.	
	21-2-17		Mil Inspection and Lecturers made up 9 tubes Spanner 31: p.DONNETS POST and	
	22-2-17		moved up. During much 10.40 a my 9th w. 2 Div'n 9 S.n.B permet 31: p ..... D.2 DONNETS POST	
	23-2-17		-do- done two a free reference t.b.	B"	
	24-2-17		-do-	3	
	25-2-17		-do-		
	26-2-17	9 ... a.m.	Bn moved to trenches with Em infantry of Batt Rose to operate taking ..... over the front between, A' DONNETS POST	
	27-2-17		-do- Bn ... Physical Training + Lown touch.	P. DONNETS POST	
	28-2-17		Arms Rill. Bn duty cont. ..... & Coy 9 Co.	B"	

E.M.Mur Cap
Comd 54th Bn

WAR DIARY FEB 1917

Appendix I

The task allotted to 54 M.G COY was as follows:—
2 Guns to each of the assaulting Battalions.
4 " in the Bank at R.32.B.99 for strong Points
which were to go forward after the final objective had been won. These
Guns were to man the strong points.

The orders given to the two Guns going forward with the 11th R. FUSILIERS
were:—

To go forward with the 4th Company. The right hand Gun was to
watch for any gaps between the N. HANTS & the R. FUSILIERS & the other to watch
the flank between the 53rd & 54th Brigade. The left hand Gun with this
Battalion experienced slight difficulty in getting to within 80 yds of SOUTH MIRAMOUNT
TRENCH & by sweeping this Trench with M.G fire it considerably assisted the FUSILIER
Party. It continued firing until the Infantry had withdrawn & returned at
about 8.30 a.m. Only 2 of en of Gun Team were left to bring back the Gun &
Tripod. The other Gun with the FUSILIERS was held up at SOUTH MIRAMOUNT
Trench for about 20 mins.

It then pushed on & greatly assisted the Adjutant of the
FUSILIERS by coming forward through heavy M.G & Rifle fire to take up
position in what the Adjutant described as a "very weak line". Only one
Man of this Team survived.

The two Guns with the right assaulting Battalion had orders to
watch the right flank but experienced no difficulty in pushing right
forward to S. MIRAMOUNT TRENCH where under the leadership of Lieut PRICE they
helped to form a defensive flank facing East along the WEST MIRAMOUNT ROAD
When Lieut PRICE decided to withdraw they covered his retirement & came back
themselves into a position on the W. MIRAMOUNT ROAD at R.11.B.2.6.

Owing to our right flank being so exposed it was decided to
push forward the 4 Guns in the Bank at R.22.B.99. This would be about 9.30 a.m.
These Guns got into position without a casualty & had no opportunity of getting
any targets.

It was decided shortly afterwards to take up a defensive position
8 Guns were placed:— 2 in No 2 strong point. 2 at 11C 44 (approx)
3 at 11D.2.6 (approx)   1 at 11C.65 & 1 at 11D.34

The other 8 Guns of this Company took up a position on the
evening of Feb. 15th in O.C.I North of Louchy way with orders to fire on Targets at
R.3.B.5.6. to R.4.B.25 (4 Guns) & R.3.D.29 to R.4.A.53.

On the 17th these Guns opened fire on their Targets & carried on from 5.45 a.m
till 10 a.m. This fire was evidently effective as a message was received from Division
also from the ESSEX REGT. that considerable annoyance was being caused by Bosche
Guns situated in trench R.4.A.53. to R.4.D.53. — that is to say from a spot
commencing from where one of our Targets left off.

The 8 Guns were immediately brought to bear on this target & continued
firing until 6 p.m.

No further trouble was reported from this Quarter.

Nov/4
March 1917

CONFIDENTIAL

WAR DIARY

OF

54 MACHINE GUN COMPANY

FROM 1st MARCH 1917.   TO 32nd MARCH 1917.

WAR DIARY or INTELLIGENCE SUMMARY

Army Form C. 2118.

(Erase heading not required.)

Instructions regarding War Diaries and Intelligence Summaries are contained in F.S. Regs., Part II. and the Staff Manual respectively. Title Pages will be prepared in manuscript.

Place	Date	Hour	Summary of Events and Information	Remarks and references to Appendices
BUZINCOURT AUTHILLE	1-3-17	9.15 a.m.	Coy. paraded at 9.15 a.m. & marched to AUTHILLE. Rebel Tents are on rising unbroken ground, overlooking the Ancre about 5:30 pm.	
	2-3-17		Paraded at 10:30 a.m. & proceeded to AUTHILLE to assist tents, packed previous day.	
	3-3-17	9 a.m.	Coy. leaves Authille accompanying the 11.6 Coy. redrawing a Flat B. Log. and orders for movement of Ranges	
	4-3-17	9 a.m.	Coy. marched to 9 sections, 9 refreshments of Lark. Arrived 3:30 pm. Strength of 140 OR's provided to the BARS	
	5-3-17	9 a.m.	Wood parties round. A few unable from BENNETS POST. 13 p.a.	
	6-3-17	9 a.m.	Repr. from Copy. T Clearing of Camp.	
	7-3-17	9 a.m.	Wire road & drawing up tents march.	
	8-3-17	9 a.m.	Coy. employed for erecting ranges concentrator sumps in Camp.	
	9-3-17	9 a.m.	_ditto_ _ditto_ _ditto_	
	10-3-17	9 a.m.	The whole Company employed erecting Theatre.	
	11-3-17	9 a.m.	Special parties of Clergy &c. on Sunday. 6 on 9 inspection of buildings.	
	12-3-17	9 a.m.	Whole Company on Theatre. Paraded at 5 p.m. & proceeded to MIRAMONT & IRLES via Bucquoy Rd. No. 53 N.G Coy in the Buc	
	13-3-17	9 a.m.	ACHIET LE PETIT Line reported evacuated. Coms. ordered to push forward with infantry to occupy evacuated trenches. About 9 am. 2 Secs. of 2. Section ordered forwards to MIDDX. advance forests on STAR ROAD. 2 Secs of D/2as. went forward to ACHIET-GREVILLERS, taking up positions in conformity with support div.	
	14-3-17	10 a.m.	No attack was made on the BUHUCOURT line. D/2as. going further forward who gave covering fire to advancing Troops. So attack showing that Coms. were withdrawing to original positions.	
	15-3-17		No change during the night several of the guns and Coms. light mode. gave the track over stopping further advance to tracks & roads leading from ACHIET-LE-PETIT. ACHIET LE GRAND & BIHUCOURT	
	16-3-17		No 1 Sec. of 2. Sec. pushed forward with the MIDDLESEY to occupy BIHUCOURT. 2 Secs. went up in position in front of the village the other No remaining at Battalion HQ.	
	17-3-17		D/2as. went forward with advance guard through BIHUCOURT to BEHAGNIES - ERWILLERS road & took up positions in conformity with advance Div. 'B' Sec. with Y/ BEDFORDS pushed forward & occupied the BUHUCOURT line	
	18-3-17		D/2as. moved forward with the advance guard & advanced to ST LEDGER & took up positions for defence of the village. C/2as. march to ERVILLERS. B/2as. Secs. were withdrawn & the 9 gun gull into Bucks at BUHUCOURT	
	19-3-17		Attack on CROISILLES by 6th HANTS. 3 of D/2as Secs. gave covering fire. the 4th Secs. being placed & positions in reserve. left flank attack was unsuccessful & infantry withdrew to original positions. D Sec. moved forward to ERVILLERS	
	20-3-17		2 Secs. B/C/2as arrived to MORY with section of MORY 2 with C/Coy R. NUSILIERS, 2 on MORY-VRAUCOURT road 9.2 in advance N/o MORY	
	21-3-17	11 a.m.	Relief commenced by D. & Y. F. O. Coy D/2as. 9.2 Secs. of C. relieved & returned to Bucks at BUHUCOURT	
	22-3-17		This Company sent 2 Sun Teams left BUHUCOURT & marched back to MARLBOROUGH HUTS. 2 Teams of B. & 2 of C. relieved other Secs. & that night met at BUHUCOURT. Proceeded the pieces the Company at MARL. HUTS.	
	22-3-17	7:15 a.m.	Coy. paraded & fell marching order & proceeded to CONTAY & reported on roll by Supt. Comments. Coms. billeted in billets about 4 p.m. The three remaining Secs. Teams arrived CONTAY about 10:15 P.M. after a very long march.	
	23-3-17	9 a.m.	Left CONTAY & marched for VILLERS BOCAGE arriving about 1:45 pm.	
	24-3-17		Entrained at VILLERS BOCAGE detrained at REVILLERS & billeted at 6:15 pm.	
	25-3-17	1.45	Paraded at 10:15 am. & marched to BACOUEL station. Four more explosions arrived this mg & entrain until 6:30 the following morning.	

WAR DIARY or INTELLIGENCE SUMMARY

Army Form C. 2118.

Place	Date	Hour	Summary of Events and Information	Remarks and references to Appendices
THIENNES	26-3-17	6.30 a.m	Entrained at BACQUEL station departing at 7.25 a.m.	
	27-3-17		Detrained at BERGUETTE about 1.30 p.m. After being warmed with Tea & Rations, Bty marched to THIENNES	
	28-3-17		Cleaning of Guns & material. Unpacking of limbers	
	29-3-17	9-10 a.m	Gun Drill. Removal of Kit & fitting of asbestos clothing	
	30-3-17		do	
	31-3-17		do	

J.E. Strong Lt. for Capt.
Comdg. 54 S.B. Bty.

Vol 15

WAR DIARY

OF

54 MACHINE GUN COMPANY

FROM, 1st April 1917.

TO, 30th April 1917.

Army Form C. 2118.

WAR DIARY
or
INTELLIGENCE SUMMARY
(Erase heading not required.)

Instructions regarding War Diaries and Intelligence Summaries are contained in F. S. Regs., Part II. and the Staff Manual respectively. Title Pages will be prepared in manuscript.

Place	Date	Hour	Summary of Events and Information	Remarks and references to Appendices
THIENNES	1/4/17		Church Parade in forenoon and Inspection by Commanding Officer in afternoon.	
	2/4/17	8.30 a.m.	Company Parade for Battle. 2 p.m. to 5 p.m. fitting & testing of Box respirators.	
	3/4/17		Heavy fall of Snow. Cleaning Guns & packing limbers in Garrison. Redistribution & checking of spare parts.	
	4/4/17		Arms Drill & Physical Drill in the forenoon. In the afternoon Box respirators drill.	
	5/4/17		Arms Drill & Physical Drill. Practice alarm in the afternoon.	
	6/4/17		Route March in forenoon. In the afternoon Generals Gun Tests (Pte Chapman 1 Pl)	
	7/4/17		Arms Drill & Physical Drill in the Garrison & the afternoon Box respirators.	
	8/4/17		Church Services. Lombered Wagon Competition.	
	9/4/17		Arms Drill & Physical Training. Company Drill in afternoon.	
	10/4/17		Physical Training. Route March.	
	11/4/17		Arms Drill & Physical Training. Cleaning guns.	
	12/4/17		Scheme at NEPPE FOREST	
	13/4/17		Arms Drill & Physical Training	
	14/4/17		Route March. Football.	
	15/4/17		Church Services & Inspection of Billets.	
	16/4/17		Physical Training and Gun drill. & Proclamation in am.	
	17/4/17		Brigade day. Cancelled owing to wet weather. Cleaning guns.	
	18/4/17		Baths for Company and Commanding Officers inspection.	
	19/4/17		Lui gun teams "A" "B" "C" on aeroplane drill. Remainder of Company cleaning guns	
	20/4/17		Mg gun teams of Section "D" & "G" reinforcement for aeroplane duty at FORT Hdq	
LE PIRE	21/4/17		Company moved off at 7.30 a.m. from Thiennes and arrived at 5.30 a.m. & rested at 6.30 p.m.	
	22/4/17		Company Parade 9.15 am gun cleaning.	
	23/4/17		Outpost scheme at ALLOWARKS Company moved off at 5.30 am & returned at 6.30 pm	
	24/4/17		Parade 9am killing Belts. Parade for Bath 2.30 pm	
	25/4/17		Parade 9 am Gun Drill. Mechanism & Aimed Drill.	

WAR DIARY
or
INTELLIGENCE SUMMARY

(Erase heading not required.)

Army Form C. 2118.

Place	Date	Hour	Summary of Events and Information	Remarks and references to Appendices
LE PIRE	26/4/17		2nd Section. Packing up for moving. Company moved off at 1 a.m. arrived at SACHIN at 5.45 p.m. 2nd Section carried from Aeroplane duty between 12 midnight & 3 am	
SACHIN	27/4/17		Company moved off at 5.30 am for PERNES arrived there at 9.30 am. During breakdown on line Company had to proceed to BRISSE to refuel. Company arrived at BRISSE and entrained at 4 pm for ARRAS. Arrived at ARRAS at 10.30 pm and marched to trenches outside NEUVILLE VITASSE arriving at 12 midnight.	
NEUVILLE VITASSE	28/4/17		Brigade conference at 10 am. attended by Lieut C.J.C. CODD. Captain E.C.T.MINET having reported sick. Reconnaissance of trenches by Acting C/O Lieut C.J.C. CODD. "A" Section moved into trenches at 7.30 pm. to relieve 21 Machine Gun Company.	
—	29/4/17		Gun cleaning from 10 to 12 noon. "B" Section moved into reserve at 4.30 pm Company H.Qrs moved up the line at 4.30 pm. to N.9 CENTRAL.	
—	30/4/17		"C" and "D" Section. Cleaning guns. Postman Knight E. wounded outside NEVILLE VITASSE about 6.30 pm.	

Suthafield
10/5/17

C J Clodd Lt
Comm 54 Machine Gun Coy

Vol 16

CONFIDENTIAL

WAR DIARY

OF

54 MACHINE GUN COMPANY

FROM, 1st Jan, 1917
TO, 31st May, 1917

WAR DIARY
or
INTELLIGENCE SUMMARY

(Erase heading not required.)

Army Form C. 2118

Place	Date	Hour	Summary of Events and Information	Remarks and references to Appendices
NEUVILLE VITASSE	1		In trenches at NEUVILLE VITASSE awaiting orders for moving up the line.	
	2		Brigade Conference & Company Conference. Nos. 14 & 15 Gun Teams moved up the line to Company H.Qrs. Nos. 13 & 16 Gun Teams reported to Divisional R.E. C' Section moved up to front line. Positions taken up about 12 midnight.	SEE APPENDIX 1. for 3rd & 4th
	3		Attack commenced at 3.45 a.m.	
	4		Relief commenced by 53 M Gun Company at 7.30 a.m. Completed 10 p.m. Returning to trenches at NEUVILLE VITASSE	
	5		Cleaning guns & packing limbers from 2 to 5 p.m. Parade for bath from 5. 6. 6.30 p.m.	
	6		Cleaning guns & packing limbers from 9.30 a.m. to 12.30 p.m. Parade for pay at 2.30 p.m.	
	7		One hour Arms Drill & making up shortages. Kit inspection by Section officers at 4 p.m.	
	8		One hour Arms Drill. Inspection of clothing by Section officers.	
	9		One hour Arms Drill. Elementary Training.	
	10		Physical Training. Arms Drill & Gun Drill.	
	11		One hour Arms Drill & Route March.	
	12		Preparation for moving. Cleaning guns. Checking spare parts to packing limbers.	
N.3.1.C.	13		Moved from NEUVILLE VITASSE to N.3.1.C. Construction of bivouacs. Transport moved from BURAINS to BOIRY ST. MARK. Parade for pay in afternoon.	
	14		Construction & completion of bivouacs. Making latrines & washing places. Construction of cooks house.	
	15		One hour Arms Drill. Physical Training. Range finding.	
	16		One hour Arms Drill. Physical Training. Short Route March.	
	17		One hour Arms Drill. Physical Training. Gun Drill.	
	18		One hour Arms Drill. Tactical handling in the open.	
	19		One hour about Drill. Range finding & musketry.	
	20			

2449 Wt. W14957/M90 750,000 1/16 J.B.C. & A. Forms/C.2118/12

Army Form C. 2118.

WAR DIARY
or
INTELLIGENCE SUMMARY
(Erase heading not required.)

Place	Date	Hour	Summary of Events and Information	Remarks and references to Appendices
N 31 C.	21		One hours Arms Drill. Brigade Scheme. Visit to Sports.	
	22		Heavy Rain all day. Parades cancelled. Parade for pay at 3pm.	
	23		Brigade Field day. Practising the attack.	
	24		Arms Drill. Musketry. Range Finding.	
	25		Arms Drill. Physical Training & Musketry.	
	26		Arms Drill. Tactical handling in open warfare.	
	27		Service for R.C. Company at Baths.	
	28		Arms Drill. Physical Training. Gun Drill. Parade for pay.	
	29		Tactical handling. Taking up positions from map references.	
	30		Brigade Field day. Practising the attack.	
	31		Arms Drill. Remainder of Day occupied with Company Sports.	
In the field 10/9/17				

Signature
Comdg 54 Machine Gun Company

APPENDIX No 1

Notes on attack 3/4 May 1917

On the night of 2nd May 1917 "A" Section with four guns was holding Brigade front and "B" Section with four guns was in support.

"C" Section moved up from NEUVILLE VITASSE and two guns under 2/Lieut PATON reported to C/o 12th Middlesex Regt and two guns under 2/Lieut CUMMINS reported to C/o Bedford Regt. Two gun teams of "D" Section reported to O/c 79 R.E. Field Co with orders to go forward and occupy strong points as soon as the infantry advance should make their constructing possible. One gun team of "A" Section which had been withdrawn from front line owing to Brigade on our right taking over a portion of our front was also detailed for holding a strong point. Remaining two guns teams of "D" Section reported to O/c 80th R.E. Field Co with orders to hold two forward strong points which his company was detailed to construct when possible.

The teams detailed to report to the assaulting battalion and also those for the strong points have been made up to 8 men per team the extra men being furnished by the reserve battalions. This enabled each gun team to have ten belt boxes and one petrol tin of water in addition to shades, condensers &c.

The attack commenced at 3.45 a.m and "C" Section went forward with the infantry H.Q. wave.

The left gun was put out of action and the bulk of the team knocked out by an enemy machine gun which had been in hiding when the infantry went forward. The next gun narrowly missed the same fate and was rendered useless by a rifle bullet which perforated the barrel casing and also the breech. Several of the team were wounded and the survivors subsequently got back to our lines with the gun. The next gun most of the team were knocked out by shell fire. The right hand gun also suffered from shell fire two men only returning with the tripod. It is presumed that the gun and the rest of the team were knocked out.

The survivors of "C" Section were collected and sent back to

APPENDIX No 1 (Continued.)

to the reserve line.

An hour after Zero the two left guns of "A" Section went forward to the crest and did good work by giving covering fire for advancing troops and also by enfilading enemy trenches. Your guns of "A" Section and two of "D" Section remained in this line until relieved the following night by 53 M. Gun Coy.

E. Millett Capt
Comdg 54 Machine Gun Coy.

In the field
10/6/17

Vol 17

CONFIDENTIAL

WAR DIARY

OF

54 MACHINE GUN COMPANY

FROM 1st June 1917

TO 30th June 1917

WAR DIARY or INTELLIGENCE SUMMARY

(Erase heading not required.)

Army Form C. 2118.

Instructions regarding War Diaries and Intelligence Summaries are contained in F. S. Regs., Part II and the Staff Manual respectively. Title Pages will be prepared in manuscript.

Place	Date	Hour	Summary of Events and Information	Remarks and references to Appendices
N 31 C	1.		In the forenoon ½ Company cleaning guns & ½ company at bath. In the afternoon the company paraded by sections to the range.	
	2.		Making preparations for move into trenches. Packing limbers &c.	
			Stripping leavage & making final preparations for the move into trenches. Company paraded by sections at 8 a.m. moved off in sections at 15 m.t. intervals. Before relief was completed a raid was made by the Enemy on a forward gap of the front line when one of our gun teams had taken up a position. We lost one gun.	
HINDENBURG SUPPORT	3.		Relief completed at 10·15 p.m.	
	4.		In trenches. Situation normal.	
	5.		do	
	6.		do	
	7.		do	
	8.		do	
	9.		do	
	10.		Sections C & D carried out inter-relief. Remainder unchanged.	
	11.		do	
	12.		do	
	13.		do	
	14.		Gas discharged with good effect	
	15.		do	
	16.		Relieved by 158 M.G. Coy. Relief carried out without hindrance from the Enemy & Completed at 11-15 p.m. The company camping at BOISLEUX ST MARC	

WAR DIARY
or
INTELLIGENCE SUMMARY

(Erase heading not required.)

Army Form C. 2118.

Place	Date	Hour	Summary of Events and Information	Remarks and references to Appendices
MONCHY-AU-BOIS	17		Company paraded for baths & change of clothing. In the afternoon packing of lorries to	
	18		Company paraded at 4 a.m. & marched to MONCHY-AU-BOIS arriving about 6-30 a.m. Company rested at this point for the day. Paraded at 8-45 p.m. & marched to Huts (George 4) P+S	
P+S	19		Company arrived at Huts (George 4) about 1-30 a.m. Kit inspection 11 a.m. Inspection of Company by C.O. at 2-30 p.m.	
	20		Cleaning guns & looking times	
	21		Tactical Scheme. Company parade for bay.	
	22		Physical Training. Gun Drill & Aim Drill	
	23		Selection of positions. Communication between guns. Clearing the P+S GRENAS road as a trench	
	24		Church parade & Tournoien & Kit inspection at 12 noon by Section Officers.	
	25		Reconnoitering for a short range for practice purposes	
	26		Digging of gun Emplacement S.E. of bomb Range. Sect. Practice & Revolver practice	
	27		from 9 to 10 a.m. Physical Training. From 10 to 12 noon Ammo Drill & Company Drill. From 12 noon to 1 p.m. Advanced gun drill. Company parade for bay. (U Sect. Range practice 1. Star Revolver practice.)	Range practice 12 Revolver practice on 11th 21st 23rd
	28		9 to 10 a.m. Box Respirator Drill. 10 to 12 noon Bombing & laying & setting of guns to excellent dust fair	
	29		Paraded at 3.45 a.m. for range at MONCHY-AU-BOIS. Arriving about 9-15 a.m. Practices 8, 9, 14, 9, 13 days firing commenced about 11 a.m. & continued to about 8-30 p.m.	
MONCHY-AU-BOIS			of Part II Table Cleven carried out. Firing commenced about 11 a.m. & continued to about 8-30 p.m. Returning to billets at BIENVILLERS after a most successful days shooting	
	30		Paraded at 4 a.m. marched to Camp at P+S arriving at 6.30 a.m. Remainder of day men were allowed to rest as attend divisional sports	My Powell

CONFIDENTIAL

WAR DIARY

— OF —

54 MACHINE GUN COMPANY.

FROM 1st July 1917   TO. 31st July 1917

WAR DIARY or INTELLIGENCE SUMMARY

Army Form C. 2118.

(Erase heading not required.)

Instructions regarding War Diaries and Intelligence Summaries are contained in F.S. Regs., Part II. and the Staff Manual respectively. Title Pages will be prepared in manuscript.

Place	Date	Hour	Summary of Events and Information	Remarks and references to Appendices
CANAL RESERVE CAMP (H.29.7.5.6)	1st		Company standing to awaiting orders. Rained heavily the whole day.	
	2nd		Still ramming. Vickers gun teams of Sections "C" & "B" succeeded to the 8th Station Essex and 7th N.S. Cy in the line.	
	3rd		Still raining. Vickers gun teams of C & D Sections returned to Camdes at 9am, for consolidation of relief of 98th M.G.Cy. Gun teams	
	4th		No 2 boat completely knocked out owing to trenches	
	5th		A Section & Gun Team of Section 'B' & C Gun Teams of Section D moved to CHATEAU SEGARD at 8pm.	
	6th		General Routine work. Nothing unusual to report.	
	7th		" Guns on point line examined & released	
	7th		A Section moved to DORMY HOUSE. Fire Teams of 'B' Section relieved the 17th Bn Bedfordshire Regt	
	8th		4 x 6 Guns of 'B' Section moved with 11th Bn Royal Fusiliers to RITZ AREA	
	9th		Attack which was to have taken place postponed on account of bad weather conditions. Heavy fall of rain.	
	10th		Attack on GLENCORSE WOOD and INVERNESS COPSE by 51st Infantry Brigade (WESTHOEK RIDGE)	APPENDIX I
	11th		Severe shelling of new positions assembled. No heavy casualties to the division. Relief commenced by 53 M.G. Cy. First	
	12th		gun team arriving at CANAL RESERVE CAMP about 5am.	
			Relief still in progress and not completed till about 2.30am. The last of the gun teams arriving leaving at 8.30 am.	
			Bus arranged for moving. Busses pulled in at Canal Reserve Camp at 11am. Bus 3.5am and 29 at 8.55am on route for	
			STEENVOORDE arriving at 6.10pm. Thereat 9.15 remainder of Company bussed & opened at 6.30pm	
STEENVOORDE	13th		Company ordered for baths and issue of clothing. Returns of men, N.C.O officer for pay.	
	14th		Preparation of Company and Gun Cleaning.	
	15th		Shot route march in forenoon. Examination shooting of gun parts re. Ankles received at 12 M.N. for Company to proceed	
AT ABEELE	16th		Company handed at 4.30am and marched to ABEELE STATION where they entrained. Detrained at ARNEKE at 12.30pm and marched to BUYSSCHEURE arriving at 3.5pm.	
BUYSSCHEURE	17th		Company paraded at 9.30am for issue of Small Box Boats and Ammunition	

2449 Wt. W14957/M90 750,000 1/16 J.B.C. & A. Forms/C.2118/12

WAR DIARY or INTELLIGENCE SUMMARY

Army Form C. 2118.

Place	Date	Hour	Summary of Events and Information	Remarks and references to Appendices
BUYSSCHEURE	18th		Routine work in vicinity of billet	
	19th		Company paraded at 10 am and proceeded by lorries to camp at EPERLECQUES arriving at 1 pm. After drawing tea the Company commenced setting up new camp, being at billets BUYSSCHEURE at 7 pm.	
	20		Cleaned arms, manual practise inside in billets.	
	21		Physical training in pyjamas - Musical round walk in billets.	
	22		Proceeded to camp at EPERLECQUES (by lorries) at 8.30 am arriving about 11 am. Commenced return journey about 3.30 pm. Halted at ST OMER from 4.30 pm to 7 pm. Left STOMER at 7.15 pm arriving at billets at 8.45 pm.	
	23		Small tactical scheme on parade ground	
	24		Physical training. Box respirator drill by company & section	
	25		S.O.C. inspection at 11-15 am. The S.O.C. expressed himself as highly pleased with turn out of the Company. Coy. being very satisfactory.	
	26		Church Parade. Company paraded at 11.15 am for temple registered at Water. Remainder at ease.	
	27		The tactical scheme arranged for to day had to be postponed on account of weather. Company rest day employed to schedule in billets	
	28		Company paraded at 8.15 am parading in new vogues, at 9 am ready formed off, fall out being to keep from gale. Seasons had again to be postponed. Biggar's ??? placements in hands. Quiet night filling sandbags again.	
	29		Heavy rain again prevented the carrying out of scheme today. 7.15 am 'Lecture' by Co on the formation of an attack relieved in the field by the Previous Course. 10.30 am Firing Box Respirators. 11.15 am Lecture by Coy on Infantry Training.	
	30		Fallen in the general S.o.ph. Button by C/O on an examination of the Company. Platoons Company paraded at 8.45 am to carry out tactical scheme at EPERLECQUES encampment. Our army transferred was carried out Instructions & action in billets & general routine work	
	31		Paraded at 8.45 am & proceeded to camp at EPERLECQUES arriving at 10.30 am. Battalion dispersed at 12 pm. Carried on billet about 5.30 pm. Company was stood at ease.)	

Alf Turner Lt R Fy

APPENDIX. I.

MAP.REF. ZILLEBEKE. SHEETS 28 N.W.4 & N.E.3 (Parts of) EDITION 6A.

The attack on GLENCORSE WOOD and INVERNESS COPSE was carried out by this Brigade on a two Battalion front. The 7th Bn Bedfordshire Regt on the left and the 11th Bn. Royal Fusiliers on the right. Two of this Company's guns went over with the 4th Company of each assaulting Battalion. The guns with the left Battalion owing to the Division on left not having come up and a large gap having taken place between the right Battalion held out in GLENCORSE WOOD with a Company of the 7th Bn Bedfords with a 500 yard flank on both sides for 24 hours (Positions J.14.A.7.9. J.14.A.). The two guns with the 11th Bn R Fusiliers reached the RAILWAY LINE in J.14.A. Eight guns went forward to strong points but owing to the 11th R. Fusiliers falling back from FITZCLARENCE FARM to CLAPHAM JUNCTION, four of these guns were withdrawn to our original front line in SURBITON VILLAS.

As a gap had occurred between the 11th R Fusiliers and 53rd Brigade on our right 2 guns were placed to cover this with a Company of the 12th Bn Middlesex Regt. Owing to the heavy shelling 2 guns were knocked out, leaving the Company with 8. Two of these 8 were on the left, 2 in Strong Point at J.14.A.3.2. one at CLAPHAM JUNCTION and one at J.13.D.7.3. Two were left in our original line about SURBITON VILLAS. These 6 guns had very good targets the whole day as Germans continued to mass for counter attacks. We had at each gun position 30 Belt Boxes and these were augmented by 30 more. No counter attack was launched on the 10th but at early dawn on the 11th after the Infantry of the Brigade had been relieved the Germans launched a counter attack re-taking part of the Strong Point. The two Company guns remained in their portion of the Strong Point at J.14.A.3.2. and were instrumental in holding the counter attack up on the right. The enemy reached their original front line between the Strong Point and GLENCORSE WOOD but were promptly driven out. The Infantry attacking under a Machine Gun Barrage from 4 guns firing from the SURBITON VILLAS line. The two guns that were originally there and two withdrawn from (1) CLAPHAM JUNCTION and (2) STIRLING CASTLE

Vol 19

CONFIDENTIAL

WAR DIARY

OF

54 COMPANY MACHINE GUN CORPS

FROM. 1st August 1917.   TO. 31st August 1917.

WAR DIARY or INTELLIGENCE SUMMARY

Army Form C. 2118.

Place	Date	Hour	Summary of Events and Information	Remarks and references to Appendices
PAS	1		Cleaning guns & Belt filling	
	2		Preparations for moving	
	3		Company paraded at 4.30 am & marched to N. STATION. DOULLENS, arriving at 8.45 am Breakfast served. Entrained at 9.30 am & arrived at GODWARVELDT about 6.30 pm	
GODWARVELDT	4		Routine work at billets	
	5		Do.	
	6		Do. "B" Section paraded at 2.15 am & proceeded to OUDERDOM to rehears a Section of 90th M.G. Coy on aerial duties. Remainder of company physical training & Lectures on methods of indirect fire. Sections A.D.C.&D. paraded at 4.40 pm with transport & marched to DICKIEBUSCH arriving about 9.15 pm. Company held up for 15 minutes near RENINGHELST to allow KING's car to pass	
DICKIEBUSCH	7		Cleaning of camp which was in a filthy condition	
	8		All parades cancelled owing to rain. Making anti-aircraft emplacement. Afternoon lectures on contact fire	
	9		"C" Section to ammunition Trenches. Remainder of company physical training & Arms Drill	
	10		"D" Section to ammunition Trenches. Remainder of company physical training & Arms Drill	
	11		"A" Section viewed model trench system outside OUDERDOM. Remainder of company routine work	
	12		Physical training. Stripping & Stoppages. Gun drill	
	13	8.2.6	Fatigue party of 50 men carrying S.A.A. to front line Trenches	
	14		Fatigue party of 50 men digging trench (Very wet tonight) in RITZ AREA	

WAR DIARY or INTELLIGENCE SUMMARY

Army Form C. 2118.

Place	Date	Hour	Summary of Events and Information	Remarks and references to Appendices
DICKEBUSCH	15		Fatigue party of 30 men digging trenches in RITZ AREA.	
	16		Fatigue party of 50 men digging emplacements for forthcoming attack	
	17		Fatigue party 4/5 men digging trenches & emplacements do	
	18		Do Do	
	19		50 men at work on trenches MORITZ AREA.	
	20		20 men at work on trenches. 5 casualties	
	21		Preparations for moving	
	22		Relieved by 9th & 9th Coy at 9-3 am (less "B" Sect "B" Section relieved by 22nd M & Coy	
WHIPPENHOEK	23		Marched to WHIPPENHOEK (DARLINGTON CAMP) arriving about 12 noon. Inspection of belts & thorough overhaul of gear & material	
WINNEZEELE	24		Paraded at 7-30 am & marched to STEENVOORDE & from there to WINNEZEELE. T.24.a.23 arriving at billets about 11-45 am.	
	25		Heavy rain in forenoon. In afternoon changing blacking buckles	
	26		Lecture & demonstration in packing of guns, Lewis & on mules	
	27		Rautins work on billets	
	28		Physical training & preparations for moving	
	29		Paraded at 5-15 am & marched to WHIPPENHOEK. Caught in heavy downfall of rain previous to	
WHIPPENHOEK			Entering camp. Paraded again at 8-20 & marched to DICKEBUSCH HUTS arriving about 1-15 p.m.	
DICKEBUSCH HUTS				

WAR DIARY or INTELLIGENCE SUMMARY

Army Form C. 2118.

(Erase heading not required.)

Place	Date	Hour	Summary of Events and Information	Remarks and references to Appendices
CANAL RESERVE CAMP	30		Reached at 9.30 pm moved to CANAL RESERVE CAMP (+27.35.c.1.) 2 gun teams of 'B' Section reported to 11/R Fusiliers at 9.45 p.m prior to move to CHATEAU SEGARD AREA by 30th DIVISION	
	31.		Gun teams attacked to infantry units for attack launched commenced at 3.50 am 2 gun teams of 'A' Section left with 7th Queens at 6 am. 2 gun teams of 'A' Section left with 13th Middlesex at 7-30 am. 2 gun teams of 'D' Section left with 6 N. Hants at 8 am. Owing to the 30th Division failing to take their objective 54th Infantry Brigade orders temporarily cancelled & the various units returned to their former billets at the reserve camp	

In the field
9/8/17

N. Hickman Lieut
for O/C 54 Machine Gun Coy

WAR DIARY or INTELLIGENCE SUMMARY

Army Form C. 2118

54 M/C Coy.   Vol 20

Place	Date	Hour	Summary of Events and Information	Remarks and references to Appendices
BUYSSCHEURE	1st		Company paraded at 8.45 a.m. Forenoon occupied in cleaning Guns & Belt filling. Company parade for Baths in the afternoon.	
	2nd		Preparations for move to new training area. Packing limbers &c.	
	3rd		Cleaning up grounds & billets &c. Company moved off at 1.40 p.m. Marched via ARNEKE to LEDRINGHEM	
LEDRINGHEM	4th	8.45 am to 1 pm	Physical Training & Mansers digging	
	5th		Company paraded at 8.45 a.m. Physical Training, Arms Drill, Revolver Shooting & Box Respirator Drill	
	6th	8.15 and 1 pm	Selection of gun positions in the open. Rifle competition at 5 PER SECTION. Competitors emerged	
	7th		by motor lorries leaving at 6 am. Results very good. Company conveyed by motor lorries to range at ZERMEZEELE leaving at 9 a.m. arriving at 11.15 am. Firing did not commence till 1 pm, continued till 2.30 pm. After which the Company had tea & returned at 3.30 p.m. arriving in billets at 5.30 pm.	
	8th		The Company paraded at 8.15 am & proceeded to HOUTON to take part in Gas Cloud Demonstration	
	9th		The Company paraded at 9 a.m. A tactical scheme occupied the day up to 1 pm.	
	10th	7 am	'B' Section detailed with 6th Bn. Northampton Regt. practising attack New formation. 12 o'clock 3 sections carried out a small tactical scheme N.E. of billets.	
	11th		Parade day devoted to Company Sports, which went cause ? went ? very pleasant day was spent by all concerned.	
	12th	7 pm	Company paraded to Cinema. Each section taking on a fighting limber, poles, a tactical scheme was carried out.	
	13th	9 am	Selection of gun positions in the open, & digging in. In the afternoon Baths at BROUCKERQUE.	
	14th		Company paraded at 8.30 for Range. Embussed at 9.15 am. Arrived at ZERMEZEELE at 11.30 am. Firing commenced at 12.15 pm. Shoot finished at 2.30 pm. The shooting was much better than on previous days. The Company arrived back at billets at 5.15 pm.	
	15th	9 pm	The Company turned out for a demonstration on the use of Very Lights. A Section detailed with O.C. Bedfordshire Regt. to Inspect new formation of attack. Remainder of Coy in for instruction	

Army Form C. 2118

WAR DIARY
or
INTELLIGENCE SUMMARY
(Erase heading not required.)

Instructions regarding War Diaries and Intelligence Summaries are contained in F.S. Regs., Part II. and the Staff Manual respectively. Title Pages will be prepared in manuscript.

Place	Date	Hour	Summary of Events and Information	Remarks and references to Appendices
LEDRINGHEM	16th		Church Services. Church of England parade 8-30am. Presbyterian parade 9-30am	
	17th	8-45am	Company paraded with all fighting lorries reached out a Scheme at Le Hoot Farm	
	18th	8-45am to 1pm	Selection & digging of Gun Emplacements	
	19th		do	
	20th	8-45am	Selection & digging of Gun Emplacements for General's Inspection. Inspection completed at 1-30pm. Photographs of the whole Company were taken by Sections afterwards. The Company proceeded to Wormhoudt for baths. Football was played in the evening	
	21st	8-45am	Filling in Gun Positions dug the previous day. League (Soccer) Football commenced at 10-30am & finished at 1-3pm. C.Section topping the Hague	
	22nd		Preparations for move to Proven. 8-30am Transport proceeded by road. 9am Advance party left by tram. Company paraded at 12-5pm marched to Arneke Station entrained at 4-40pm & detrained at Poperinghe, 12-30am. Then marched to Tunnelling Camp near St Jan der Biezen arriving at 1-40am (23rd)	
TUNNELLING CAMP	23rd	11am	General Routine work. Cleaning up Camp, Turning Tents, Sick cases &c	
	24th	8-45am	Physical Training, Saluting Drill & Gun Drill	
	25th	8-45am	Physical Training & Practice Practice	
	26th	8-45am	do	
	27th	8-45am	do	
	28th	8-45am	do	
	29th		do & Squad Drill	
	30th	8-45am	Physical Training & Practicing Stoppages with Smoke Helmets on	
			Church Services	

54/18

Vol 21

CONFIDENTIAL

WAR DIARY

OF

54 COMPANY MACHINE GUN CORPS

FROM 1st October 1917.

TO 31st October 1917.

WAR DIARY or INTELLIGENCE SUMMARY

Army Form C. 2118

(Erase heading not required.)

Instructions regarding War Diaries and Intelligence Summaries are contained in F.S. Regs., Part II. and the Staff Manual respectively. Title Pages will be prepared in manuscript.

Place	Date	Hour	Summary of Events and Information	Remarks and references to Appendices
TUNNELLING CAMP	1st		Physical training. Elementary Gun Drill. Cleaning of guns	
	2nd		Physical training & digging of Machine Gun Emplacements for batteries against the enemy crossing aerial bursts.	
			"C" & "D" Section on Divisional Scheme under A.D.S.S.O.	
	3rd		Whole Company on Divisional Scheme under A.D.S.S.O.	
	4th		Physical training & Gun Drill. Intensive Digging	
	5th		Physical training followed by visit to Model Trenches. "C" Section attached to 1st Bn. Bedfordshire Regt. practicing the attack.	
	6th		O.C. No.18 Sect. & Officer took part in attack and 8 guns attached to 1st Bn. Royal Fusiliers & 12th Bn. Middlesex Regt. O.C. No.10 & 15 under 2nd Lieut BATCHELOR attached to 6th Bn. Northamptonshire Regt. for practicing the attack. Reconnaissance of terrain. Physical training & Bathing.	
	7th		Lunch & Rounders.	
	8th	8.45am	Route march. Packing Limbers. Baths.	
	9th		Physical training. Examination of kit to be taken by the 58th Brigade in forthcoming operations. Officers visit Lumm Area.	
	10th		Physical training. Weather Parades cancelled owing to heavy rain. Preparations for move to Brandhoek.	
	11th		Company paraded & marched off at 10 am and finishing centre. Entrained at VAN DER BIEZEN for IRISH FARM, Limbers	
IRISH FARM	12th		proceeded by road. 8.30pm Company moved into trenches. Bad weather. Strong winds & rain.	
	13th		Eastern preparations between the attack on centre attack with 55th Dvn Brigade.	
TUNNELLING CAMP			Entrained at IRISH FARM at 10.45am & detrained at VAN DER BIEZEN at 12.45 on arriving at TUNNELLING CAMP about 1.15pm. After having tea the Company furnished for bath at VAN DER BIEZEN at 2.30. All ranks had a very enjoyable evening & was best in Margate	
	14th		Company paraded at 9.45am on orders dress for fitting of clothing. Remainder of day spent in cleaning of equipment. Company paraded at 9 am in Gross dress for reorganisation of Sections. Cleaning of equipment.	
	15th		Company paraded at 9.30am & marched to Entrance to Camp at POPERINGHE-PROVEN ROAD. From there to	
	16th		BRIELEN, thence marched to IRISH FARM. Reconnaissance of gun positions made by C.O. & two Officers on horseback.	
IRISH FARM	17th		Proceeded to road to lines at CHATEAU DES TROIS TOURS.	
			Working party detailed for move into trenches. Company proceeded to trenches at 2.30pm. 15 minutes interval between "A" & "B" Section, "C" Section. Company battle W.O.C. at PALACE FARM. Relieved 53 Machine Gun Company. Relief complete at 8.30pm.	
	18th		1 case of W.O. Eight guns in the line. More deserted at company H.Q. Relief & Rear Telling & look out at the Trenches.	
			Lenses of A Section relieved 2 teams of A Section at the fort. Going to Rear Telling & look out at the Trenches.	
			Did not be shot at Company H.Q. until 1-30 am. "D" Section organising swords emplacements over front line	

1875 Wt: W593/826 1,000,000 4/15 J.B.C. & A. A.D.S.S./Forms/C. 2118.

Army Form C. 2118

WAR DIARY
or
INTELLIGENCE SUMMARY
(Erase heading not required.)

Instructions regarding War Diaries and Intelligence Summaries are contained in F. S. Regs., Part II. and the Staff Manual respectively. Title Pages will be prepared in manuscript.

Place	Date	Hour	Summary of Events and Information	Remarks and references to Appendices
IRISH FARM	19th		"C" Section relieved 2 gun teams of "A" Section in the trench. On arrival at Company HQtrs the mobilization should have been completed by 6 p.m. and not completed until 8 a.m. owing to heavy shelling of the back areas by Boche. Brigadier making alterations in our front line.	
CHATEAU DE TROIS TOURS	20th		Relieved by 58 Machine Gun Coy. Relieving company arrived at Company HQtrs about 4 p.m. but owing to heavy shelling of back area could not proceed further until about 6.30 a.m. Relief completed about 7 p.m. "C" Section proceeded to TUNNELLERS CAMP. Band reliefs of success taken on limbers at IRISH FARM to CHATEAU DE TROIS TOURS arriving about 7 p.m.	
	21st		Regt. gun proceeded to Brooks Rd. Range for Section practice.	
	22nd		The company less "A" Section & 1 gun team at CHATEAU DE TROIS TOURS	
IRISH FARM	23rd		"C" Section 8 gun teams arrived at CHATEAU DE TROIS TOURS at 10 a.m. The company marched by foot to IRISH FARM arriving about 3.30 p.m. Ten gun teams paraded at 5.30 p.m. to report to Brooks. Orders received and Chief report and training practices of Headquarters Coy Cavalry skilled.	
	24th		7 gun teams left IRISH FARM at 2.45 a.m. for trenches to relieve 58 Machine Gun Coy. Orders received for transport to leave from CHATEAU DE TROIS TOURS to DIRTY BUCKET CAMP.	
	25th		Relieved. 20 6 Machine Gun Coy. 7 gun teams marched independently to CANAL BANK via No 4 BRIDGE under Hy. shellfire and for DIRTY BUCKET CAMP.	
DIRTY BUCKET CAMP	26th		Company paraded for bath & change of clothing. Remainder of day spent in cleaning up. Heavy rain.	
	27th		Company paraded at 7.15 a.m. for inspection. Remainder of day spent in cleaning guns &c.	
	28th		Company paraded at 9.30 a.m. for misters. Voluntary Church Service. Refreshments, framers.	
	29th		Company paraded at 11 a.m. marched to PARTRIDGE CAMP arriving about 3.30 p.m.	
PARTRIDGE CAMP	30th		Company paraded at 9.15 a.m. Reorganized. Digest of information by O. C. Section. Remainder of day.	
	31st		Physical training. Kit Inspection. Squad Drill	

J. E. Strang Lieut & Adjt.

Vol 22

CONFIDENTIAL

WAR DIARY

— OF —

54 COMPANY MACHINE GUN CORPS

FROM 1st November 1917.   TO 30th November 1917.

WAR DIARY or INTELLIGENCE SUMMARY

Army Form C. 2118

(Erase heading not required.)

Instructions regarding War Diaries and Intelligence Summaries are contained in F. S. Regs., Part II. and the Staff Manual respectively. Title Pages will be prepared in manuscript.

Place	Date	Hour	Summary of Events and Information	Remarks and references to Appendices
PARTRIDGE CAMP	1		In the afternoon Coys cleaned & Sandbagged up tents.	
	2		Usual training. Squad Drill. Extemporising of Guns. Lumber cleaning. Sandbagging up tents.	
	3		Physical training. Box Respirator Drill. Gas Drill. Lumber parade. Bath for half.	
	4		Inspection of Company by Commanding Officer. Bath. Hiking. Bivouac pitching for escort.	
	5		Coy paraded at 11.15 then proceeded by bus from PROVEN to INTERNATIONAL CORNER & then marched to "H" Camp arriving about 12.15 pm	
H CAMP INTERNATIONAL CORNER	6		Physical training. Box Respirator Drill. Squad Drill. Special night operation Coy	
	7		Squad Drill. Box Respirator Drill. During 5 to 6 am they marched to the day & were devoted to mechanism	
	8		Squad Drill. Physical training. Digging Trenches, round huts	
	9		Making preparations for move to available area. Baths at ELVERDINGHE in afternoon	
EMILE CAMP ELVERDINGHE	10		Company less D. Section & Lambpost paraded at 2.30 am & proceeded by train to BOESINGHE. Our arrival at this point they proceeded to Trenches to relieve 53 M.G. Coy. Relief carried out without hindrance from the enemy	
			D. Section & Lambpost moved off at 9.45 am & marched to EMILE CAMP, ELVERDINGHE.	
	11		In Trenches	
	12		In Trenches. Nothing unusual to report. Preparations for inter-company relief	
	13		2 Section relief carried out today. C. Section relieved A. B. Section relieved B.	
	14		In Trenches. Situation unchanged	
	15		In Trenches. An attempted attack by the enemy on left of British Right of Sec of Coy frustrated.	
	16		In Trenches. Preparations for relief. Due to take place tomorrow.	
	17		Company relieved by 53 M.G. Coy. B. Section and Lambpost left EMILE CAMP, ELVERDINGHE at 9.45 am & marched to "H" Camp arriving from Trenches about 6.30 am. C. & D. Sections arrived at H Camp at intervals between the hours of 7.30 am & 8.30 am.	
H CAMP INTERNATIONAL CORNER	18		Gas Shoot on cleaning up. Company parade for Pay at 2 pm	
	19		General routine work from 7 am to 5 pm	
	20		Company ready for move. Physical training. Box respirator drill. Rev Section 3 in Trench from relieving	
	21		Preparations for moving tonight. 2 sections proceeded to BOESINGHE arriving at 11.3 am	

WAR DIARY or INTELLIGENCE SUMMARY

Army Form C. 2118.

(Erase heading not required.)

Place	Date	Hour	Summary of Events and Information	Remarks and references to Appendices
IN CAMP	22		Other Coys at RESINGHE proceeded to front line trenches "B" & "C" Sections to SIGNAL FARM "D" Section & Headquarters to EMILE CAMP	
EMILE CAMP	23		In trenches	
ELVERDINGHE	24		In trenches	
	25		Inter-company relief. "B" & "C" Sections relieved A & B in front line	
	26		In trenches. Casualties 1 O.R. killed	
	27		"D" Section relieved "B" & "C" Sections from in a "D" Section & part of "C" proceeded by lorries to SIGNAL FARM leaving EMILE CAMP at 1-3 pm. 2 gun teams at 2 pm. Casualties 2 O.R. killed	
	28		In trenches	
BOX CAMP A.S.C.9.1	29		Company relieved in line by 53 M.G. Coy. Relief commenced at 3-30 pm & completed without hindrance from the enemy by 11 pm. 1 gun team detained from front line & retained at RESINGHE & trained at BOX CAMP, A.S.C.9.1	
	30		Day spent in cleaning up. Baths & Pay out in afternoon	

W.R. Matthews 2/Lt
for O.Ph. 34 M.G.C.

CORRIGENDA TO OPERATION ORDER NO. 22.

ADVANCED PARTY. The Advanced Party will now consist of Lieut. H.W.Brookling and C.Q.M.Sgts. of "A", "B", "C" and "D" Coys. only.   This Party will report to Lieut. Brookling at the Headquarter Mess at 6.30 a.m. tomorrow and will proceed to ABEELE, reporting to Staff Captain at Brigade Headquarters at 8 a.m., when they will proceed by Bus to new Area.

TRANSPORT. Cancel from "Starting Point :- to LA MOTTE", and substitute :-
Brigade Transport will proceed by the WORMHOUDT - HERZEELE Road.
The Battalion Transport will join the remainder at D.7.c.3.2. at 9.30 a.m.
All arrangements as to order of march will be made by O.C., 152nd Coy. A.S.C.
The entire Battalion Transport will move off at 7.30 a.m.

26 Vol 23

CONFIDENTIAL

WAR DIARY

OF

54 COMPANY MACHINE GUN CORPS

FROM, 1st Dec 1917   TO, 31st Dec 1917

WAR DIARY or INTELLIGENCE SUMMARY

Army Form C. 2118.

(Erase heading not required.)

Instructions regarding War Diaries and Intelligence Summaries are contained in F. S. Regs., Part II. and the Staff Manual respectively. Title Pages will be prepared in manuscript.

Place	Date	Hour	Summary of Events and Information	Remarks and references to Appendices
BOX CAMP A.S.C.P.1	1st	9am	Inspection of Company by Commanding Officer. Physical training. Steaming & lamps carried to tinsmith	
	2nd	"	General Parade. Picking out defects to diminished Equipment Lists. Kit P.O.	
	3rd	9am	Physical training. Risk Regiatia. Drill & Parade Drill.	
	4th	"	Building dislocations for more thousand packs. Tenders &c.	
	5	"	Company entrained at Ordnance Station at 10am Coys proceeding to LARRY CAMP detraining at ELVEROM SHEH those going on the line detrained at MESINEH, from is not long &c. Arriving down the line proceeded by ... ... at 2am.	
LARRY CAMP PEAK M.Q.P.	6		[illegible lines]	
	7	"		
	8	"		
	9	"		
	10	"		
	11	"		
BOX CAMP A.S.C.P.1	12			
	13			
	14			
	15			
SMSMOUTH CAMP	16			
	17			
MINSHE W.A.S.S	18			
	19			
	20		Route March	

WAR DIARY
or
INTELLIGENCE SUMMARY
(Erase heading not required.)

Army Form C. 2118.

Place	Date	Hour	Summary of Events and Information	Remarks and references to Appendices
MARINE M.E. AREA M.T.M. A.S.C.	21st		Personal Drill. Squad Drill. Digging Employments & Camouflaging & Earl Nearing of Road	
	22nd		Physical Training. Box Respirator Drill. Squad Drill. Digging Employment. Road Surfacing.	
	23rd		Church Service	
	24th		G.O.C. Inspection	
	25th		Fatigue parade by Sections for baths at ROSSIGNOLS from 9am to 11am. Christmas Dinner	
	26th		Holiday	
	27th		Physical Training & Box Respirator Drill. Stripping. Squad Drill. Stoppages. Principles & Use of 2 & 3 Sections. Paraded at 8.30am. Talk on Tactical Scheme arranged by Brigade	
	28th		"A" & "C" Sections carry out usual daily programme	
			"B" Section in conjunction with 6.4/B Battalion Leinster Reg. & "D" Section 14th. H.L.I. Br. Battalion.	
			Bgt. Raft Tactics Tactical Scheme. "A" & "B" Sections carry on with daily programme.	
	29th		Church Service. Kit inspection by Section Officers Thanksgiving for most to NORMANSQUE AREA & 3 days fatigue	
	30th		Proceeded to HOULLE Company preparations to march to NORMANSQUE AREA via 3 days fatigue	
	31st		Sections consisted of at Wash & Entrained at TROIS ROIS for ST MOMELIN arriving at 18 & 19 own	
			My Detachment Transferred to HOULLE arriving at 12 midnight	

[signature]

17 WO 24

CONFIDENTIAL

WAR DIARY

OF

54 COMPANY MACHINE GUN CORPS

FROM 1st JANY.1918. TO 31st JANY.1918.

Army Form C. 2118

INTELLIGENCE SUMMARY
(Erase heading not required.)

Date	Hour	Summary of Events and Information	Remarks and references to Appendices
HOULLE			
1st		Company trying practice on range near ERERLECQUES, wo	
2nd		B. & 1/2 Section found duties in pairs. A Section cleaning ship in billets	
3rd		A Section extracts of B Section doing sanctioneroleant. Holiday for remainder of Company. Moved out	
4th		Moved off at 1.0m. En route for BOX CAMP	
		Company arrived at 6.45am. Marched to St MUNSEL. Entrained for BOX CAMP	
BOX CAMP			
5th		Westen trained to BoxCamp arriving about 2pm.	
6th		General Section work. Cleaning kit &c	
7th		Church Service. Baths for 2 Section & Remainder	
8th		Baths for remainder of Section & Headquarters. Squad Drill & Sex Rechnahr Drill	
		Educational treatment for company. Demonstration by 2 Gun teams of B Section before Brigadier-General	
		Organisation of Gun Stand for the team	
		Preparations for move out the tent Trenches 5 & machine Gun Company	
		attended. Detail at LARRY CAMP. Not carried out. Successfully	
		Visit carry't work at LARRY CAMP to personal in Trenches	
LARRY CAMP	9th		
& TRENCHES	10th	do	
	11th	3 & 4 Section relief C & B Section octang A & B Section in the Line. A Section octang to Signal Farm	
	12th	Trench. Usual neutral work at LARRY CAMP.	
	13th	do	
	14th	do	
	15th	do	
	16th	Company engaged in Tunnels by 155th In. Coy. Relief carried out with incident completed at	
	17th	9.15pm. The company returning to their old billets at BOX CAMP	
BOX CAMP	18th	Both change closing of clothes for company	
	19th	General Training. Section Drill Squad Drill & Foot Drill	
	20th	Church Service. Kit inspection by Section Officers at 12 noon	
	21st	2 Section Course't at 6.45am. By Motor Allotment of equipment carried out. Physical	
		Training. Foot Drill. Squad Drill. Sex Rechnahr & Mouth of Gun	
	22nd	Company headed by B Section at 9.05am. By Omnibuses from OIR REVSLEE to Rationia location commencing	
		with 2d Section at 9.15am. Remainder of Company marching to BOSSINGHE. Relief	
	23rd	Company paraded at 2pm. and marched SOUDAN STATION. R LARRY CAMP. A B & C Section	
		at sea at ELVERDINGHE Station. & B Section detained at BOESINGHE	

WAR DIARY
or
INTELLIGENCE SUMMARY
(Erase heading not required.)

Army Form C. 2118

Place	Date	Hour	Summary of Events and Information	Remarks and references to Appendices
B COMP	22nd	at 1.20pm	Proceeded by Sea from Forth Escadas to relieve 55 Coy Div Sigs at 2 pm	A&B Notes
			On Braeles & at SIGNAL FARM. Relief completed at 8.15 pm	
IN TRENCHES	22nd		Usual Routine work at ARMY CAMP (REAR H Q RS)	
		2.5pm	do	
		2.6pm	do	
		2 pm	do	Orders received re. orders for 3rd inst
		2.5pm	do	Brigade refused Company doing 1 extra day in the line
		2 pm	do	Company exchange of orders up 96th Br Sig'd by Visual Section at SIGNAL FARM
			Camp at 5.30 pm Relief carried out successfully, terminated about 11.30 pm	Enemy shelling at MARGATE
		3.0 "	Company moved to CROMARKE. N. Section HQRS Detail proceeded by route march arriving at 7.15 pm	
			A.B.&D Sections proceeded by lorries arriving at 12.30 am	Bombing started on telecn
			(Signal Huts) CROMBEKE at 4.35 pm	
CROMBEKE	31st		Baths & Cleaning up	

O. M. Mahrum 2 L.
for 94. 58. Dv. Signs

www.ingramcontent.com/pod-product-compliance
Lightning Source LLC
Chambersburg PA
CBHW081442160426
43193CB00013B/2359